In Praise of *The*

"*The Woman Code* is a book for ou
Through personal anecdotes, real
wisdom, Sophia Nelson shares the ways women ...
value, live authentically, and understand that a truly successful life
is shaped from the inside out."

Arianna Huffington, *New York Times* bestselling author of
Thrive; founder of *The Huffington Post* and *Thrive Global*

"*The Woman Code* is a life compass, a Code that holds to timeless
principles of faith, family, friendship, and sisterhood. It is a conversation that we need to share with our daughters and the younger
women we encounter. It will perhaps be a road map for mothers to direct their sons to seek virtuous women. Sophia has done
a powerful job of bringing it all together in one inspiring book."

Serita A. Jakes, bestselling author; director of Women's
Ministries, The Potter's House

"Sophia Nelson may be petite in stature, but inside she stands tall
and strong. Her passionate mission is to see other women empowered to be all they were created to be, and she stewards that passion
well. In this book Sophia lays out 20 keys, from being stuck in time
to finally flying free."

Sheila Walsh, bestselling author; speaker at Women of
Faith conferences

"We all encounter chapters in our lives that test us to our core.
Sophia has put together a remarkable Code for living life that will
enable modern women to face those tests and not just survive them
but thrive despite them."

Sherri Shepherd, comedian, actress, talk-show host

"Sophia Nelson is a powerful and poignant voice for women of our
time. By challenging us to unlock our inner greatness or Code, she
is calling women to live higher, to live on purpose, and to succeed
first from a deep place within."

Sunny Hostin, co-host of *The View*, ABC News senior
legal correspondent and analyst, and attorney

"As a Latina and a first-generation DREAMer, I struggled to find
opportunities and open doors to a successful career. It took many

years of trial-and-error to really find my voice. I wish *The Woman Code* existed when I was first trying to carve my own path! It's a powerful, must-read book for young women who are just starting their careers, or really anyone who wants to lead a more purposeful and prosperous life."

Daniela Pierre-Bravo, producer of MSNBC's *Morning Joe*, journalist, and co-author of *Earn It!*

"*The Woman Code* hits the nail squarely on the head! Each key and Code is exquisitely presented with authenticity and clarity. Reading this book took me back in time to situations and circumstances that I might have handled differently if only I had known better. Thank you, Sophia, for 'breaking the code' and showing all who read this book that the keys to peace of mind, self-confidence, and self-awareness lie within each of us and that no one can unlock us but ourselves."

Terri P. Dean, former chief membership officer, Girl Scouts of Eastern Pennsylvania, Girl Scouts of America

"*The Woman Code* offers the truth about living a life of fulfillment while balancing the daily pressures women confront every day to be good mothers, wives, daughters, sisters, friends, and career professionals. As a woman who wears each of these hats on a daily basis, I have experienced the struggle to find balance between setting aside time for myself and being there for the loved ones who need me the most. Women should know there is help available. We can succeed in all that we are called to do and also feed our own souls. This book is a terrific guide on how to achieve happiness by establishing boundaries that can empower women to actualize their dreams and control their own destiny."

The Honorable Stephanie Rawlings-Blake, former mayor of Baltimore

"You can regret the life you don't have, or you can live the life you do have to its greatest potential. Sophia Nelson offers the Codes to inspire women to do just that. *The Woman Code* is *the* guide every modern woman should read and then immediately share with her sisterhood."

Melanie Notkin, founder of Savvy Auntie; author of *Otherhood*

"Sophia Nelson offers us a powerful tool for 'such a time as this.' *The Woman Code* teaches us how to actualize our inherent power and to honor and value who we are (or were created to be) while living intentionally. Thank you, Sophia, for these timely instructions and needed reminder!"

Sheree Fletcher, actress, *Hollywood Exes*

"A life-changer. Quite simply, *The Woman Code* will change your life in its secret places. Sophia Nelson has written a book that is wise, knowing, and like Sophia herself—pulling no punches. With wisdom and empathy for the modern woman's balancing act, this book is both practical and inspirational. It also shows young women the keys to living a rich, full life, and Sophia reminds mature women how to be their very best. Her observations on value are profound and deeply felt. This is a transformational book that I urge all women to read and share with a woman or girl you love."

Constance White, author; former editor-in-chief of *Essence* magazine; former style reporter for *The New York Times*

"What I learned by reading *The Woman Code* is that in order for women to change the world, we first have to understand ourselves and then live out a timeless and universal Code of sisterhood, loyalty, leadership, and connection. Sophia is challenging all of us to rise to a higher standard, and I believe we can reach it and all be better together once we do."

Michelle Patterson, president of California Women's Conference; CEO of Womennetwork.com

"In my professional world, knowing the rules, applying them, and doing so with passion is the only way to survive. *The Woman Code* gives all of us the big-picture view on how to attain and maintain true success. It serves as a sort of GPS for how we as women make critical life decisions."

Eve Wright, senior vice president, legal affairs and US sports marketing at Unscriptd; author of *Life at the Speed of Passion*

"Sophia Nelson is a woman 'Taking The Lead.' Her powerful new book *The Woman Code* is a must-read that reveals specific ways each woman can thrive in her own life and leadership while connecting profoundly with other women to speed the journey forward for all of us."

Gloria Feldt, cofounder and president of Take The Lead; author of *No Excuses*

"Sophia Nelson understands women. She knows exactly what's in our baggage, and she gets why we gals are sometimes unnecessarily petty, extra loving, alive with the joy of life, or just barely making it. In *The Woman Code*, Nelson shows us how to deprogram: ignore the limits that society, menfolk, and families unwittingly put in our way so we can live joyful and truly authentic lives."

Elizabeth Wellington, staff and fashion writer,
The Philadelphia Inquirer

"*The Woman Code* connects the complexities and uniqueness of our being as women to unlock our individual and collective treasures of the future. The Code makes us realize we are like water—resilient beings who make it regardless of circumstances. This is a must-read page-turner."

April Ryan, White House correspondent for
theGrio.com; author of *The Presidency in
Black and White*

"'We as women are a gift to each other. . . . We yearn for each other as sisters.' I love this message and Sophia Nelson's book *The Woman Code* because it gets to the heart of how women can live in a more authentic, powerful, and meaningful way, without putting us all in a box that limits or constrains us. *The Woman Code* offers a specific, well-formulated code of honor to abide by, which provides gentle and loving yet firm and straight-talking guidance for how we can reach our fullest potential while also uplifting and supporting other women as we climb and grow. The book is a fabulous reminder of what we may already know deep down but have sadly failed to demonstrate and manifest in our daily lives, practices, and behaviors. A powerful and enlivening book for today's times."

Kathy Caprino, Forbes contributor;
author of *Breakdown, Breakthrough*;
founder and president of Ellia Communications, Inc.

"*The Woman Code* is more than a call to action. It provides a powerful, actionable, accessible way for any woman to rediscover the invaluable tools she already has within herself, tools that can guide any woman to the life she wants. Nelson also reminds us that a core to our Code as women is to support one another."

Karen Finney, former deputy press secretary
for First Lady Hillary Clinton; CNN
political analyst and contributor

"Following the success of *Black Woman Redefined: Dispelling Myths and Discovering Fulfillment in the Age of Michelle Obama*, which captured the zeitgeist of black women in the twenty-first century, Sophia is back with a book that addresses the challenges and opportunities before modern women. Her insight in *The Woman Code* is an important part of a growing library of tomes intent on helping women lead more fulfilling lives."

Krissah S. Thompson, managing editor
for *The Washington Post*

"*The Woman Code* is a very unique book. As a small business expert, I particularly enjoyed the professional Codes in this book. I believe Sophia has provided women with an internal road map on how to achieve our professional goals by first taking care of our personal and spiritual self."

Melinda F. Emerson, contributor to *The New York Times*
blog *You're the Boss*; bestselling author
of *Become Your Own Boss in 12 Months*

"*The Woman Code* is a book about purpose. About finding your own path and getting back up again when life knocks you down. Anybody who has sought purpose knows the road *is not linear*. You will have many ups and downs. Sophia teaches women in this book that it's how you bounce back that makes you a champion."

Shon Gables, veteran journalist and news anchor

"When Sophia speaks, it is with a voice that both roars and whispers. In her second book, *The Woman Code*, her voice, which is rooted in life experiences, helps to teach us as women how to respect ourselves, be responsible, and love one another. The 20 Codes she shares are things we innately know but often need to be reminded of. This wisdom is to be both shared and lived for ages. Yes! There is a Code."

Michel Wright, host of SiriusXM *Rhythm & View*
and *Heart & Soul*; veteran of WHUR/Howard
University 96.3

"Sophia Nelson is the perfect person to write *The Woman Code* because she authentically lives and breathes its contents all week long. The public and private encouragement she offers women on a daily, hourly basis is both shocking and provocative in that it always cuts deeper than you'd expect, especially for Washington, DC. In her own hilarious, reachable way, Sophia's realness will touch women in years to come and provide a sort of compass we all sometimes need."

Betsy Rothstein, editor, *The Daily Caller**

"*The Woman Code* is a compelling and interactive literary journey of self-reflection. Within every chapter, at some point you'll find yourself nodding affirmatively, thinking, *Yes, that's me*, as I often did. Sophia offers a refreshingly real and honest perspective on how to become the best woman you can possibly be and does so without pretense. The powerful truths interlaced throughout the book are applicable to every woman, regardless of where you may be in your life. That's part of the genius Sophia brings to *The Woman Code*. It empowers, inspires, and uplifts. This book is going to change lives."

Tara Setmayer Love, CNN political
analyst and contributor

"Sophia A. Nelson is a living testament to the power of bringing women together! Her book *The Woman Code* takes a powerful look at the career skills and life lessons women need to thrive professionally and personally. It's an empowering and inspirational must-read that transcends race, class, region, religion, and even politics."

Leslie Sanchez, CBS new political analyst/producer;
founder of Impacto Media; author of
You've Come a Long Way, Maybe

"Sophia Nelson is a powerful voice for a new generation of women seeking to lead from a place within. She knows how to combine her emotional intelligence, life experience, career savvy, and wit to help women decode and unlock a purposeful life filled with success."

Maria E. Brennan, president and CEO,
Women in Cable Telecommunications

*Sadly, Betsy Rothstein passed away in 2020 after a brave battle with ovarian cancer.

THE
Woman
CODE

20

Powerful Keys
to Unlock Your Life

Sophia A. Nelson

Health Communications, Inc.
Boca Raton, Florida

www.hcibooks.com

Library of Congress Cataloging-in-Publication Data
is available through the Library of Congress

ISBN-13: 978-07573-2398-0 (Paperback)
ISBN-10: 07573-2398-7 (Paperback)
ISBN-13: 978-07573-2408-6 (ePub)
ISBN-10: 07573-2408-8 (ePub)

Publisher: Health Communications, Inc.
        1700 NW 2nd Ave.
        Boca Raton, FL 33432-1653

Unless otherwise indicated, Scripture quotations are from the Holy Bible, New International Version®. NIV®. Copyright © 1973, 1978, 1984, 2011 by Biblica, Inc.™ Used by permission of Zondervan. All rights reserved worldwide. www.zondervan.com

Scripture labeled VOICE is taken from The Voice Bible. Copyright © 2012 Thomas Nelson, Inc. The Voice™ translation © 2012 Ecclesia Bible Society. All rights reserved.

Scripture labeled WEB is taken from the World English Bible.

The author wishes to acknowledge that she has used pseudonyms, composite characters, approximated dialogue, and some factual events out of chronological order to protect the identities of real-life persons. There is never intent to harm, embarrass, or malign these persons. Parts of this book that could be considered memoir, anecdotal, or autobiographical may be better considered creative nonfiction.

This paperback edition of the book is dedicated
to my maternal grandmother,
"Mudda"
Evelyn Marie Smith
(January 15, 1930–Still Going Strong at 91)
As a baby, and as her first and eldest grandchild,
I could not say "Mother dear" so I pronounced it Mud-da.
I still call her that to this day.
She is one of the strongest women I know.
The living embodiment of "The Woman Code" in action.
She is the matriarch of eleven children
(nine still living), over twenty grandchildren,
and a half dozen great grandchildren.

Contents

Section I The Personal Codes

Whatever is going on inside of you is what will come out of you. These four Codes are the foundation of every woman's life. All roads to positive life transformation begin with you doing the work on yourself. Self-examination is core to how we develop into the women we all want to be.

Section II The Emotional Codes

Our emotions as women are at times both a blessing and a curse. These four Codes will help women to recognize and better manage their emotions from a place of wisdom, self-reflection, self-love, and resilience.

Section III The Spiritual Codes

Every woman has a spirit. The spirit part of us is often the part we neglect most. Spirit is not religion. Spirit is not a bunch of rules. Spirit is what keeps you on track to nourish your soul and be a light to all who come across your path. These four Codes are simple, but they are powerful when put into practice in your daily life.

Section IV The Professional Codes

Successful women are intentional. They live by powerful Codes that integrate their personal, spiritual, and professional values into a winning strategy for all. They lead at work as they do at home—with heart, compassion, sisterhood, smarts, and savvy. That is what makes women unique.

Section V The Relational Codes

If COVID-19 taught us anything, we know that we are in this life together. We are connected. We need one another. No Codes determine our ultimate joy, happiness, and fulfillment in life more than the Codes for how we relate to other people. At the end of the day, it is our relationships that make our lives worth living.

"Before the moon I am,
what a woman is, a woman of power,
a woman's power, deeper than the roots of trees,
deeper than the roots of islands,
older than the Making, older than the moon."

—URSULA K. LEGUIN, Tehanu

Foreword

Why Knowing Your Value
Is Essential to The Woman Code

Mika Brzezinski, co-host of MSNBC's *Morning Joe*
New York Times bestselling author of *Know Your
Value, Earn It, and Comeback Careers*

When I first read *The Woman Code* in 2014, I was thrilled to see the first "Code" Sophia detailed and built the rest of the book upon: Know Your Value.

Anyone who knows me, or my work, knows it is my mission in life to help women recognize and celebrate their value. It is the central tenet of my own book, *Know Your Value: Women, Money, and Getting What You're Worth.*

I wrote *Know Your Value* in 2012, digging into personal stories and examining why it took so long for me to truly understand my value and communicate it effectively. I wanted to understand why we, as women, are fierce about protecting, defending, and augmenting the success of others—but when it comes to ourselves, we tend to shut down, self-deprecate, and apologize our way through the conversation. And I wanted to help us change that.

So much has happened since 2012. Hillary Clinton ran for president in 2016, followed by Kamala Harris, a woman of color, running for vice president in 2020 and winning to become the nation's first female vice president, under the nation's oldest elected president, Joe Biden.

The #MeToo movement finally forced conversations about rampant sexual assault into the mainstream. The deaths of George Floyd, Breonna Taylor, and others at the hands of police spurred a nationwide reckoning on race and how our country treats people of color.

And in 2020, the world has faced unprecedented challenges because of the coronavirus pandemic. It has hit women particularly hard personally and financially, as we juggle our roles as professionals, caretakers, mothers, and wives—simultaneously. But as women always do, we have stepped up. We have supported each other. We have practiced the "Woman Code" that Sophia wrote about so powerfully in 2014.

The re-release of *The Woman Code* in paperback could not come at a better time. More than ever, we need the lessons and inspiration that Sophia shares in her personal story from struggle to success.

In the original book introduction, Sophia shared how she had hit rock bottom after a painful break up with the man she loved, and she chronicles her journey of self-discovery: finding her authentic voice, desires, self-worth, and ability to make impactful relationships that give life purpose. It is her version of hitting the reset button after a major life setback, accepting the past and coming back stronger.

And she has translated that journey into lessons for all of us. Sophia presents her hard-won guidance through twenty tenets of the woman code: personal, emotional, spiritual, and professional. She shows how we can be resilient for ourselves and pull up one another; how we can celebrate our gifts and those of our fellow women; how we can level the playing field at work; how we can have courageous conversations in every facet of our lives.

It all begins on page one with the foundational Code: Know Your Value. This is the most essential Code for all women, from the emerging professionals entering the workforce for the first time to those of us navigating our careers and lives as we age.

Our value is our superpower. It took me years to know my value, but as Sophia and I have both found, once you get there, you will never go back. The pages to come will help you along that all-important journey, and above all else, I hope you come to own your voice—and enjoy the lifelong benefits that come when you truly know your value.

Acknowledgments

A lot has changed since I wrote the original *The Woman Code* in October 2014. The world is not the same place it was six years.

What has not changed is my amazing "front row" and the wonderful women in my family. Spanning the generations from age eighteen to ninety-one: my nieces Mikaela Lynn and her sister Alexandra Leigh; my mom, Sandria; my maternal and paternal aunts; my cousins (over thirty of us); and the family matriarch, my maternal grandmother, Evelyn.

While there are too many amazing women in my life to name in this book, I do want to send my profuse thanks to some precious ladies who sit at the forefront of my life and my heart no matter time or distance. Even if we had to untie for a minute, we've never cut and run from each others' lives. Dr. Sabrina Jackson, Soror Trish Smith, Talaya Simpson, Andrea Agnew, Soror Kimberly Reed, Soror Nicole Roberts Jones, Dee Dean, Soror TJ Haygood, Vanessa Maddox, Dani Keemer Edmond, Patrice McNeil, Rhonda Lambert Parson, Andrea Morris, Soror Lesleigh Robertson, Cheryl Carr, Soror Rev. Adriane Blair Wise, Kalpana Patel, Soror Jackie Washington, Soror Markey Pierre, Soror Katina Semien, Soror Chelle Wilson, Soror 29th Madam Supreme Dorothy Buchanan Wilson, Soror Diedra Fontaine, Soror Pastor Renee Fowler Hornbuckle, Shonny D. Young, Crystal Smith, Kate Jones, Jill Whitlow, PJ and Lauren Riner, Dishan Washington Winters, Tina Johnson, Tracy Hamlin, France Saunders, Tina Moore, Mira Lowe, Towanna Freeman, Rosalind Hudnell, Soror Colita Fairfax, and Soror Angela

Spranger. And lastly, to my little-big sisters Stephanie Lucente, Councilwoman Roxy Ndebumadu, cousin Jasmine Morton, Joy C. Smith, Rachel Hornbuckle and the beautiful Indian girl I met on the train, who is now getting an MBA at Columbia University, Impana Srikantappa, I can't wait to see what you all do in this world.

You have all blessed me with your compassion, caring, love, wisdom, and honesty, and how you daily walk out the Code of sisterhood, loyalty, friendship, and faith. You've pulled me through an incredibly challenging time in my life. You've stuck by me. You've comforted me. You've prayed for me and lifted me. You've walked out the Code without even knowing what it was. This book is likewise dedicated to all of you. I am forever in your debt. I love you and thank you. There is a Code: sisterhood.

To my trusted longtime literary agents, Claudia Menza and Leticia Gomez, thank you for sticking with me for the past decade. I am so blessed to have you two amazing women in my life. Thank you for all you do to make me shine. Thank you for being loyal and true.

Thank you to Mika Brzezinski for an amazing book Foreword. I am such a big fan of all you do, and I am so deeply humbled that you lent your name and your voice to this book. It is 100 percent about knowing your value. To Maureen Clancy and Daniela Pierre-Bravo, thanks for making it happen for me.

With much appreciation also to those who lent their names to this book's "In Praise of" section and book jacket, believed in its mission, and supported its launch. Thank you. You humble me.

My profuse gratitude to the Revell team for making the original book happen.

Thank you to my wine partner, Jennifer Breaux of Breaux Wineries, our Woman Code Wine Club (breauxvineyards.orderport.net/product-details/2957/Club-Woman-Code--Wine-Club-Membership).

Last but not least, thank you to my wonderful team at HCI, Christine Belleris, Christian Blonshine, Lori Golden, Larissa Henoch, Allison Janse, and Camilla Michael.

Prologue

Unlocking the Power of the Woman Code

Fill your life with women that empower you, that help you believe in your magic and aid them to believe in their own exceptional power and their incredible magic too. Women that believe in each other can survive anything. Women who believe in each other create armies that will win kingdoms and wars.

—Nikita Gill

Every woman lives by a Code. And her Code either propels her to greatness or keeps her stuck in the challenges and obstacles in her life.

Our Code is our compass. Our Code is what keeps us, protects us, and allows us to honor others as well as ourselves. People often ask me, "What do you mean by a Woman Code?" And I respond that it is a simple set of timeless values, virtues, and commonsense sisterly conduct that we must first practice on ourselves, and then—and only then—can we practice it with others.

Codes are core to how we develop into the women we all want to be. Codes begin in our families, for better or for worse. Our family is the birthplace of all things good and not so good. And throughout the rest of our lives, we play what I like to call "tapes in our head" of the things we heard, saw, and experienced firsthand. Family is our first school of learning. It is from our families that

1

we hope to learn the value of self. The value of truth. The value of integrity. The value of life. Of honor. Of faith. Of friendship. Of relationship. Of forgiveness. Of joy. Of sorrow. Of loss. And, most of all, of resilience.

Some of us—perhaps too many of us—did not get the positive and affirming messages from our families. Or from our childhoods. We did not come from a TV sitcom world, where all the warts were covered up behind perfect smiles and seeming tranquility. A world where viewers saw only what they were allowed to see: false perfection. False reality versus honest and true authenticity. For some of us, our families and our childhoods were not the white-picket-fence world of those sitcoms. We were not reassured, protected, loved, or nurtured. Instead, we got mixed messages about our value and our worth. We were measured against a sibling who was taller, prettier, smarter, or just more favored than us. We were told we were not good enough, that we would never amount to anything special. We had to fight for Mom or Dad's attention, or, worse, we were often never acknowledged by them at all.

And that, my fellow sisters, is where self-doubt begins. That is where competition with other women begins. That is why so many of us, at some point in our lives, find ourselves feeling a little lost, adrift, unsure of who we are, and what, if any, value we have in the world. I wrote this book to help us find our way. To help us remember that we have this amazing power inside of us as women. It just has to be unlocked. Unleashed. Freed. And given permission to take root in our day-to-day living, working, caring, healing, sharing, and respecting of other women.

As for me, I learned much of my Code from my paternal grandmother. She was a beautiful woman physically, of mixed race, and an even more beautiful woman inside. She only completed junior high school, which was not uncommon in her day. And she had a hard life: a child of the Great Depression, she had to work to help her family. She missed out on her own dream of becoming a nurse. Instead, she raised three children alone, working odd jobs, cleaning people's houses. Her children never did without. I adored her. She was authentic. She was brave. She was accountable. And she was so very resilient.

What I miss most about her is not just her wit and wisdom but her unconditional love for me. I was her firstborn grandchild, and she made sure I knew that she was proud of me. She got to see me graduate from law school. Be sworn into the Bar as an attorney. I look like her. I am tough like she was. I walk by her Woman Code, the one she modeled to me every day until she died in September 2000.

So you see, this book is not based on theory or research. It is based on *living*. It was birthed from a place of deep self-discovery after I had endured even deeper pain. When all is said and done, we are accountable for our lives and our choices. We often look at the things and the people that have hurt us, and we get stuck there. I was feeling sorry for myself, when what I needed to be doing was learning about myself. Once I came out of my hurt place and found my liberated place, the words just poured out of me. *The Woman Code* was born from the cleansing rawness of grief that, once it has run its course, provides unimaginable clarity.

Throughout the annals of time, we women have often given voice to our pain through the power of the pen, putting our discoveries into words so that other women can learn from our missteps as well as from the things we get right. In that vein, I hope that you will learn—from me and the women's stories that I share throughout this book—that life truly is a journey, whether you are in your late teens or twenties, in midlife, or in your golden years. You are the keeper of your heart's desires. You are the one you have been waiting for. In my wallet I keep the words from the old Nike ad: "It's never too late to have a life. And never too late to change one." That is what living is all about.

This is a book about truly knowing, loving, and honoring yourself as a woman. This is a book about self-worth—how we treat ourselves and how we teach other people to treat us. This is a book about protecting your heart yet being brave enough to love unconditionally. This is a book about your past, and how you need to make peace with it so you can move toward all that lies ahead of you and all that is yet to manifest within you.

This is a book about learning to live authentically. Credibly. Boldly. And with a heart that is wide open yet guarded wisely at the same time.

This is a book about acceptance and how freeing it is to our souls. About grace, being accountable to yourself and to others, and learning how to embrace the gift of aging gracefully—because to age is to be alive and being alive is a gift.

This is a book about resilience and how to unlock the power within you to face anything life throws your way. Things will happen to you that will knock the wind out of you. But you must get back up again and again. In this book you will learn that, even amid your worst struggles, you will inevitably stumble across your strength.

In short, I have come to tell you that you, my sisters, are a gift. Because no matter what life throws at you or takes from you, when you know your value and your worth, nothing is impossible.

The truth is, we women spend much of our time looking outside ourselves for the answers to life's questions. That is the wrong place to look. There are times when life will block your view and you must stand up so you can see clearly. But everything you need to win in life is right inside you. That is my message to women. Stop looking outside yourself for validation. Stop looking outside yourself for your healing. Stop looking outside yourself for your faith, for your fulfillment, for your deepest desires. *They are sleeping inside you.* Sleeping but not dead. Waiting to be unlocked and unveiled to the world.

This is also a book that reminds us what not to do to other women in the global, spiritual, sacred sisterhood of women. The Woman Code dictates that we do not gossip about other women, punish them, or menace their reputations even when they hurt us. We wish them well and we commit to do them no harm. In truth, what makes us amazing as women is that we lift other women as we climb. We do not deny when we are wrong, and we apologize quickly so as not to allow deep, impenetrable agony and damage to take root. We learn to choose our words wisely, even when we are angry, because we know that words can be forgiven but never forgotten.

> The truth is we women spend much of our time looking outside ourselves for the answers to life's questions. That is the wrong place to look.

We learn that sometimes we need to "cut" and sometimes we simply need to "untie" from people we once loved, trusted, and valued, leaving room for time to do its work and for growth and maturity to set in. Sometimes, by untying we can restore, rebuild, and renew those ties. But if we cut, we must be prepared to deal with the collateral damage and unfinished business that is always left behind.

This is a book that helps us to discover reserves of strength we never knew we had. It helps us in the workplace to be better employees, colleagues, managers, and leaders. It teaches us to lead from a place within: a place of empathy, compassion, loyalty, and emotional intelligence. It reminds us that we are women, and that being a woman never means we must act like or think like a man.

And most of all, this is a book about relationships and how we build them. How we attract the right people into our lives and keep them there. It is about how we reconnect with ourselves and have courageous conversations with people we love, allowing them to be heard and ourselves to hear them. It is a guide on how to genuinely love and be loved. How to remain loyal and steadfast. And, lastly, how to bring more laughter into your life, because time is so short and life is so precious—something that all of us around the world learned during the terrible COVID pandemic of 2020.

As you begin this journey into The Woman Code, I thank you for picking up this updated paperback version of the book. When the first edition was published in October 2014, I had no idea that the simple values my grandmother taught me would resonate with girls and women throughout the world. It started in Atlanta, Georgia, when Bishop T.D. and Lady Serita Ann Jakes had me as a featured speaker at their famous "Woman, Thou Art Loosed!" conference. In Canada, China, France, Africa, the U.K., and even as far as Australia, where I had the honor of speaking to a packed Sydney Opera House in 2017, this book, these values, have reached women from all walks of life. This book is close to my heart because through it I have been able to touch the hearts of women literally all over the world. It has led to discussions in book clubs, church study groups, corporate conferences, and corporate affinity group events, collegiate conferences, Hollywood women's events, global prayer calls, and even a line of wines "For the Woman's Soul," from my beloved home state of Virginia's famed Breaux Winery located in Loudoun County.

At the end of the day, sisters, we get only one life. Just one. So we must live it to the fullest.

If the unforgettable year of 2020 has taught us anything, it is that we are fragile and that we need one another. It taught us the power of taking care of one another. Of slowing down. Of paying attention to what truly matters in this life: people.

We learned about the power of sharing our food, our money, our homes. And we

> If the unforgettable year of 2020 has taught us anything, it is that we are fragile and that we need one another. It taught us the power of taking care of one another. Of slowing down. Of paying attention to what truly matters in this life: people.

learned to face our fears by holding on tighter to our faith. Our hearts beat as one global community. We learned to stop moving so fast and instead move more deliberately. We learned to take stock of what we have versus all that we may have lost. We reconnected with our parents, if even through a glass window. We hosted drive-by birthday parties in decorated trucks with music blasting.

We learned how to "Zoom" when we could not see one another at the office. We had to cancel weddings. We could not bury our loved ones properly or even say goodbye. But we survived through it all. Women were the soul of what kept the world going. We kept our families, our companies, our communities, and our nations intact. And the good news is, despite it all, we have thrived.

As we enter this new frontier beyond 2020, we are better. We are stronger. And I pray to God that we are wiser for all we have been through. Thank you again for picking up this special book. I am grateful for you, and humbled by your sisterly love. I look forward to reconnecting with the global sisterhood that made this book one of the top inspirational books ever penned.

May God bless and keep you.

Yours in sisterhood,

How to Use This Book

I am so excited for you to be reading this revised version of *The Woman Code* in paperback. There is a new prologue; each Code has a new inspirational quote and introduction; the section dividers are updated; and the Study Guide has been revised.

As you turn the pages of this book, you will see references throughout to God and the Bible. I make it no secret that I am a woman of deep faith. Your belief system may be different. And that's okay. Even if you claim no belief system at all, you surely hold to a set of principles that guides your life. Most of us, though, do believe in a force greater than ourselves, no matter what we call it. And this force is timeless and universal, like the Codes themselves.

You will see in each Code that I use what I call "keys" to unlock the power of the Code we are discussing. Everyone knows that a key is needed to decipher, unlock, or discover the message of a Code. That is what this book is all about: discovery. At the end of each chapter is a section called "Living the Code," in which I wrap up that Code with how we can live it day to day and share it with other women. The key words that end each Code are words that you should focus on in your living. You should journal the words, study them, and try to honor them. For example, if one of the key words in a chapter is Truth, think of what your truth looks like. How do you live it out each day?

There is an updated Study Guide at the back of the book that you can use in your book clubs, church groups, social media and Zoom chats, sorority groups, and corporate affinity groups.

Although you can read these Codes in any order you choose, I recommend you read them in order the first time. I have written them so that each one flows into the next, at times referencing previous Codes. Later, when you need a refresher course on one Code in particular (as we all do at times), you can skip right to that one. Whatever you do, absolutely read Code 1: Know Your Value first, because all the other Codes depend upon knowing your value.

Why the Code Matters

There is something majestic inside of you. To be a woman is to be power in motion. It is to love. It is to teach. It is to feel. It is to be a builder of life. This is a book about unlocking what lies inside you as a woman. Unlocking your Code. Learning the Code.

I searched high and low, reading about the virtues of life: faith, love, compassion, kindness, gratitude, community, connection, and so on. I used some of these virtues as undergirding principles for the Codes I share with you. Some of this is not new, but we all need to be reminded of what matters in life, particularly; after the year that was 2020; a year that will be talked about by historians, politicians, academics, researchers, mental-health professionals, and scientists for centuries to come.

I wrote these Codes as verbs, not nouns, meaning you must put them into practice for them to work in your day-to-day living. This is a book about all women. It is about what unites us as an ancient yet modern sisterhood. It is about doing the hard work on ourselves first so that we can reap the benefits of living well later.

This book is special. It is special to me because it has helped tens of thousands of women all over the globe to reconnect with their Code, with their inner power, and with like-minded women who also share the Code and flourish because of it.

There is a Code. It's time for you to tap into yours!

Section I

The Personal Codes

Whatever is going on inside of you is what will come out of you. These four Codes are the foundation of every woman's life. All roads to positive life transformation begin with you doing the work on yourself. Self-examination is core to how we develop into the women we all want to be.

Code 1

Know Your Value

No one can make you feel inferior without your consent.

—Eleanor Roosevelt

Y ou are the only person on this earth who can make you feel
less than or inferior. It does not matter what others say about
you, think about you, or do not like about you. It only matters what
you think about you. Neither your family's definition of you nor
unkind words spoken to you are valid.

Value is another way of saying "worth." Value is another way of
saying "importance." Value is another way of saying "precious."
You and you alone must define yourself—for yourself. You must
love and like you or no one else ever will. It is life changing to know
your value. One of the most timeless and challenging issues for
women of every generation is the struggle to know our value, to
know our worth, and to claim what we deserve in the workplace
and in our relationships.

Knowing your value means not only knowing who you are but
who you are not. I know that some of you may not feel very valuable
right now, or very loved. That is okay. That is why you picked up
this book. Many women look good on the outside but are badly
wounded on the inside. They may seem successful, but they are

13

hiding their hurts inside. Believe it or not, they feel valueless too. So I need you to stop thinking you are alone. You are not. Every single one of us at some point has doubted her value.

Women today are educated, talented, connected, financially secure, gifted, well traveled, and more, yet we still do not know our value. We shrink from saying what needs to be said for fear we will be called the "B" word or worse. We fear outshining men lest we make them feel less than. We worry that we are not pretty enough, smart enough, talented enough, or powerful enough. We envy other women who are thinner, more beautiful, smarter, or happier. We fail to see the amazing gifts we are to the world.

It is time for that to change.

All of our doubts, fears, and limitations come from within our own minds. Envy starts out as admiration. We want what other women have because we don't see our own intrinsic value. We are so good at advocating for and empowering other people but not ourselves. We know how to negotiate a fierce deal for a client, and we will go to the mat for a family member or friend when we feel someone is not treating them as they deserve. Yet we will diminish our own value; we do not stand up for ourselves and honor our worth.

We can possess an Ivy League degree and an amazing work history, and yet when it comes time to negotiate for that salary at the new job we just landed, we let someone else decide our value. *Men never do this.* From the time they are boys, men are empowered by their families, their culture, their communities, and even the sports teams they play on to know their value. Men are taught almost from birth that they are to be hunters, protectors, providers, and winners. In other words, they have value.

This is not the case for us.

Women are taught almost from birth that we are to be nurturers, supporters, encouragers, peacekeepers, and ladies. While these are all great virtues, these traits play into what we call "soft skills." Soft skills, which most women possess in abundance, are important; however, they do not often get you what you want when it comes to the corporate boardroom, business, or life. How you value yourself has a direct impact on how well you live out your Code.

In a nutshell: your life "Code" is formed from the time you are a small girl. It is shaped by the influence of your parents and your nuclear family. And after the family, it is shaped by your community, by the friendships you form, and by the faith (or spiritual value system or lack thereof) your parents impart to you. Your Code either propels you to greatness or keeps you stuck in the challenges and obstacles of your life. If you grow up in a family of people who are nurturing, loving, and kind you are more likely as an adult to *be* nurturing, loving, and kind. On the other hand, if you grow up in a family where people are angry all the time, argumentative, and demeaning to one another, you are likely to handle conflict as an adult by arguing, demeaning, and yelling at people.

All women struggle with self-esteem, self-worth, and self-value issues. Women have been taught for centuries that we are second-class citizens. It is not easy to undo centuries of programming. But we are going to consider three keys to unlock how to know and honor your value as a woman.

1. Erase the negative tapes in your head—don't let your history define your destiny.
2. Realize that what you think about you is what others will think about you.
3. Shift your thinking to put you at the top of your list.

Erase the Negative Tapes in Your Head—Don't Let Your History Define Your Destiny

Words have power. Words define, shape, and mold us beyond what we can ever imagine. You have value. You are born and created as a person of value. How you perceive your worth and self-value is shaped by your experiences. And once certain words and images have been placed in our spirit, it becomes almost impossible to redefine ourselves so that we can truly embrace our value.

One of the most fundamental factors that determines your happiness, success, and joy in life is how well you value yourself. It sounds simple, but far too many women and girls do not know their value. You must be defined first and foremost by your Creator and yourself.

> Words have power. Words define, shape, and mold us beyond what we can ever imagine.

The bottom line is this: if you let others define you and tell you your value, your journey in life will be hard, passionless, and unfulfilling. We are defined early on by our families, the first place we learn how to be, who to be, and what we can be. It does not matter whether we were raised by two loving parents, a grandparent, a beloved aunt, or even in foster care. What matters is what these loved ones or caretakers spoke into our being. The power of words spoken over us, about us, and into us can last a lifetime. Words have the power to inspire, propel, or diminish us.

All women, regardless of our geographical region, nationality, religion, or socioeconomic status, grew up being defined by labels. How you value yourself was determined by how your nuclear family spoke to you, spoke about you, and how they saw you. My labels were as follows: *Sophia is my smart one. She is going to be an attorney. She is my talker. She is outgoing. Sophia is a real go-getter.*

Those words were ingrained in my Code early on. They were for the most part affirming words. I honored the high value bar that was set for me by my family. I grew up to be an attorney. I am still outgoing and a go-getter. But I had friends who did not get affirming labels. They were called fat, unruly, worthless, shy, average, boy crazed, too introverted, and worse. Many of the girls I grew up with became women who lived out the value that was placed on them by their families. It is the rare woman (e.g., Oprah) who can overcome the negativity of her early life and rise above the labels that shattered her Code. But, *it can be done* when we are given the tools to go within and dare to love ourselves again.

Two Women, Two Different Stories

Janet is forty-four, never married, and has no children. She is a successful civil engineer. Janet grew up poor in a small town in West Virginia. Like many in her community, she grew up with a strong religious faith, with a small nuclear family, and with a father who worked twelve hours a day in the coal mines. Her mother, Patricia, was a homemaker and took care of Janet and her three younger brothers. Everything in Janet's upbringing told her that her value was found in being a wife and a mother, and in being compassionate to other people before herself.

Janet's father was a decent man, but he drank a lot. And when he drank, he often verbally abused his children and at times physically abused his wife. Janet's father adored her. He would tell her that it wasn't her fault God made her a girl. He would tell her that she would grow up, meet a local boy, get married after high school, and start her own family. Janet knew from the time she was small that she did not want that type of life.

The mixed messages Janet got about the value of a woman, a wife, and a mother led her to decide early in her life that she never wanted to marry or have children. Janet is strikingly beautiful, yet if you talk to Janet privately, she will tell you that she feels unattractive and never quite good enough, and that she still has nightmares about her childhood.

Here's the point: Janet's instincts told her that life had more to offer her than what she saw growing up. But the negative tapes, the messages, and the words that defined Janet's value as a girl and ultimately as a woman have played in her head for years. *Don't miss this.* Janet on the outside is a beautiful, successful, smart engineer.

But on the inside, she still struggles with intimacy and relationships with men. She has pushed away some very good men because she fears that she will not be enough or that somehow they will not see her value. She closed off the doors to her heart long ago.

Donna, age thirty-four, on the other hand, heard very different messages about her value. The oldest of three children, Donna is an oncologist. Her parents were both physicians, and her sister and brother both became physicians. Donna's parents instilled in their children that they could do anything, be anything, and change anything in life they wanted to.

Donna's friends adore her. She is always the life of the party, the laughter that fills up the room, and she is an encourager to all who know and meet her. She's young, she's vibrant, and she never finishes a round with her patients without giving them a hug, a hand squeeze, or even a kiss on the forehead.

Donna's husband is a college professor. Not only do they value themselves, but they are both committed to instilling value in others. Donna exudes confidence, love, competence, connection, and empathy because she values herself. Both Donna and Janet are smart, accomplished, beautiful women who are at the top of their game professionally. Donna grew up understanding her value. Everyone around her affirmed that she was valuable. Janet grew up having to fight her way past the negative tapes and words that made her feel *valueless*. She made a success of her life but at a deep personal cost. She is afraid to love and afraid to connect.

These two women—one older, one younger—teach us something important. They teach us that how we see our value as girls has a lasting impact on how we value ourselves as women. And that once we leave the environments we grew up in, we have to reprogram any negative thoughts, words, or images that made us feel worthless, unlovable, and not valuable. What I'm saying is this: you have to fight for your value. You have to return to that core Code that you were born with that says you are worthy, you are loved, and you are valuable.

Realize That What You Think about You Is What Others Will Think about You

What does it mean to "know" something?

To know something is to be sure of, certain of, firm and aware of it. It means you are not guessing; you are informed. It means you believe it with all your might.

What does it mean to "value" something?

To value is to hold dear. To place in high esteem. To love. To adore. To commit. To see someone's or something's worth. To treasure and to protect something of priceless value. So to "know" your "value" is to simply believe that you are priceless, made from the beginning to be special, rare, to have purpose, and to be loved.

Here's the thing: when we can learn to operate in that space of self-love, self-worth, and self-value, we can soar to heights unimaginable. We can forge a universal sisterhood so great that we can truly ignite a spark that lights the way and changes the world. Feeling valuable allows us to do valuable things in life. If you don't love you, no one else on this earth can love you. That is a hard truth, because we realize that most women who lack self-love and self-esteem feel that way because they were taught to feel that way about themselves. They kept playing those negative tapes over and over again, and ultimately they believed them. Women who rise above their beginnings and mis-definitions of value are whole, complete, and fulfilled because they tapped back into their worth.

A point will come when you need to ask yourself three important but hard questions. Remember, it is never too late to believe in your value.

> Question 1: Who do I want to be? Not in terms of my achievements or position in life, but according to my core value system. What will my living say to others about who I am?
>
> Question 2: What is my life's purpose? What gifts do I possess that will make an impact that will last far beyond my life?

Question 3: What do I want for my happiness and fulfillment? What do I desire for me?

Only you can answer these questions. By answering them, you tap into your Code. And when you discover that Code, you will experience a freedom and a joy many women will never know. Your Code is the road map to your life's purpose and fulfillment.

Shift Your Thinking to Put You at the Top of Your List

Everything we do or will not do in life starts with the first Code: Know Your Value. If your Code has been corrupted you have to reset and restore it to begin anew. Realizing who we are and what we have to offer this life is a precious thing. It is a gift every woman should give herself. Believing in our value is no small task. But the reward is nothing short of miraculous. In other words, you must shift your thinking to put you at the top of your list.

You are valuable. How do you shift your thinking and recognize your value? These five steps will help you do just that; that is, they will help you value yourself and make sure that others around you know your value too.

Step 1: Trust yourself and your instincts. They are rarely ever wrong. Women have always practiced being still and listening. We are the original purveyors of "instinct" or "intuition." Listen to your inner voice. It will lead you to your purpose, to your value.

Step 2: Spend quality time getting to know you. Not your family's version of you, or your friend's opinion of you, or your boyfriend's or spouse's opinion of you. You must get intimately acquainted with you. Get to know what you like, what you do not like, and what you want versus what you need. You need to sit with yourself and pray for yourself.

Step 3: Face you to fix you. Face the wrong definitions you have been given about yourself. Families define us by our birth order, our siblings, and our traits: *she's the kind one, she's the tall one, she's the smart one, she's the bad one, she's the dumb one, she's the fat one.* The Code you have within never lies; let it help you find and face the authentic you.

Step 4: Believe in yourself. If you do not believe in you, no one else will. You teach people how to treat you (see Code 3). If people pick up that you don't like you or that you don't believe you are valuable, they will move on without you. People notice people who feel confident and good about themselves.

Step 5: Honor yourself. You know what lies in the deepest reaches of your heart and soul. You hear that small, still voice saying, "This is the way; walk in it." If you will honor what you know to be true for you, about you, and in spite of you at times, you will always honor your worth, your value, and your gifts. We lose this most important aspect of the Code when we let others define, mis-define, and tell us who we are. Stop. You were not designed by your Creator to do anything but to be you.

Living the Code

Make these ten points of wisdom part of your life this week, this month, this year.

Points of Wisdom

1. Your value comes from your Creator, not your parents, siblings, friends, or naysayers.
2. To know your value, you must practice good health. Your health impacts your emotions, spirit, and self-worth.

3. Words define value. Be intentional about those you allow to speak into your life.
4. Knowing your value directly impacts the quality of your life.
5. Knowing your value helps you to set important boundaries.
6. Knowing your value means you do not allow anyone to diminish you, your worth, or your hopes.
7. Surround yourself with people who affirm, adore, and love you deeply.
8. Have the courage to speak up for yourself. This communicates to others that you know your value.
9. When you know who you are, you are eager to spend time with you, alone, in the presence of your spirit and of your Creator.
10. Knowing your value means that you like yourself. You embrace you, even in all of your imperfection. You would choose you as a friend.

🗝 Key Words

Know	Rediscover	YOU
Value	Tapes	Embrace
Code	Affirmation	Priceless
Creator	Worth	Woman

Code
2

Make Peace with Your Past

Think about any attachments that are depleting your emotional reserves. Consider letting them go.

—Oprah Winfrey

I f I could go back and talk to my younger self, I would tell her to make peace with all of the things that have hurt her, made her feel unloved, or made her feel less than. I would tell her that if she does not learn to let those things go in her twenties, she will still be struggling with their residue in her fifties. I would tell her that she is strong, she is kind, and that she is going to be okay. She can, and will, be better down the road if she does the work. The truth is, we cannot change what has hurt us in the past. And we cannot fix it either. We must decide to do the work to heal from it, learn from it, and move on more wisely.

One of the hardest things to do is let go of those things that are behind us. No matter how old we get or how many roads we have traveled, we all remember, regret, and look back. This is human. Our pasts have valuable lessons to teach us if we are willing to learn and put them into the proper perspective. Yet, to stay stuck in the past keeps us from moving forward. You are not defined by your past. But your past has something to teach you.

Think of it this way: You are sitting in your car. You have a spacious view through your windshield. Hanging at the top of the windshield is a small rearview mirror. The window in front of you is wide; it allows you to see everything ahead of you so that you don't miss what is down the road. Yet the rearview mirror only allows you to see what is behind, and with such a limited, distant view.

Do you ever wonder why the view through the windshield ahead is so large and the view through the rearview mirror is so small? It's because what is ahead of you is what is most important. What is behind you only needs to be viewed once in a while. Hence, the goal of our lives, Sisters of the Code, is to keep focused forward and not look back. Living life forward is how you want to live.

In this Code we are going to look at four keys to unlock how we get past our past.

1. Recognize that you are stuck in the past.
2. Accept what you cannot change.
3. Discover how to release regret.
4. Learn how to turn your pain into purpose.

Too much of what we do is exterior. By "exterior" I mean that we are always looking for the answers, the script, and the power that reside outside of us. Respectfully, Sisters, that is the wrong place to look. Everything you need, everything you can be, everything you desire rests inside you. You are a gift to the world. We all have it inside. But very few of us know how to tap into our "Code." When we begin to accept that we are enough, our lives will shift in ways unimagined.

> Everything you need, everything you can be, everything you desire rests inside you.

By unlocking what is already inside you, you create a pathway for success in all of life—mind, body, and soul.

If you dare to find the courage to face your past, deal with it, and lay it to rest, you can move forward daringly into all life has for you. I like to say, "You have to face it to fix it." I live by a Code, just like all of you. But this particular Code (making peace with my past) has been difficult for me. I am an adult child of an alcoholic (by the way, we are all adult children of *something*). And although that label does not define me, it informs me about the things I have to be mindful of in my walk. It informs me that my Code has suffered a *little damage*. But Code can be rewritten. Yours and mine. It all starts with a willingness to be accountable. It starts by taking inventory of what we need to keep and what we need to get rid of.

Recognize That You Are Stuck in the Past

The first step to making peace with your past is to recognize that you have not yet done so. Here are a few questions to ask yourself:

- Do you find that you still feel anger, sadness, guilt, or hurt when you reflect on certain life events?
- Do you constantly think about what you missed, what you lost, what is behind you, or what or who has hurt you?
- Do certain people from your past still have the power to make you feel pain at the mention of their name or on sight of their image?

If the answer to any of these questions is YES, then you are stuck in your past. Your past still has power over you. Before I go any further, let me say something important: believe it or not, you can be stuck on good things in your life that need to be placed on the shelf. For example, some people were superstars in high school or college, but once they graduated, life didn't go so well for them. Those people often talk about the "good ole days." They live life looking backward. They live life full of regret. Of *would've, could've, should've*. Every one of us knows someone like this. Sadly, some of us are these people.

Sometimes we get stuck. We wake up and our twenties are behind us. Our thirties roll by, and then come our forties. Life happens. Family members age and die. Relationships end. Friends leave. Jobs change. We marry. We divorce. We have children or we don't. We have great joys and deep sorrows. Before you know it, it's time to retire. We wonder what we've missed. We feel so limited by time. We feel limited by what we "missed." When in reality, we never have to miss anything.

Please hear what I just said, Sisters of the Code. *You never have to miss a thing you want in life*, and here's why: If you, like me, are a woman of faith, then you are familiar with a great Scripture in Joel 2:25, which promises that God can restore the years that have been lost. And he can. But in order for him to do so, we need to do our part. And our part begins with a cleansing. Every once in a while we need a good "soul detox." A "detox" helps us to get rid of the residue that life can deposit in our souls. Not letting go of the past is a big residue builder in our lives. And it's time we released what we can no longer rectify or restore and move forward to what lies in front of us.

Residue is a word I want you to keep in mind because residue corrupts your Code. Residue is like a bathtub ring. Residue is caused by damaged relationships, a wounded inner child, people who walk out on you, unforgiveness, anger, bitterness, and the wear and tear of life. No matter how we resolve (or do not resolve) life's issues, we are always LEFT with a RESIDUE.

No matter what you are facing right now, or what happened to you last week, last month, or last year, DO NOT allow that to become a RESIDUE. Do not allow yourself to become broken by someone else's brokenness. Every time we push love or friendship away, it isn't because we don't want it but because we cannot receive it. When people hurt you, use you, or discard you, it's likely they do so because it has been done to them first.

If you are stuck in your past, the good news is that you picked up this book, and that means you want more. You want to unlock what you know has been buried inside you far too long. Yes, your faith will help get you there. Yes, your true friends will cheer you on. And yes, your family will be there, if you are lucky, to comfort you. But at the end of the day, Sisters, you and you alone must make the choice to release the pain of your past and move forward into your future.

Accept What You Cannot Change

Dealing with the demons of your past starts from a place of acceptance. Without acceptance we can never move past what has hurt us. "God, grant me the serenity to accept the things I cannot change, courage to change the things I can, and wisdom to know the difference." This prayer, "The Serenity Prayer," hangs in my bathroom; it is the first thing I see each morning. I first learned this prayer as a nineteen-year-old college student attending my first Al-Anon meeting in San Diego, California. It has helped me through some rough patches in my life.

Acceptance can only come after we have gone through the stages of grieving. Acceptance helps to bring us peace; to see something as it really IS, not as we may want it to be. Acceptance also opens up new possibilities. It allows us to release, to close the door on the past, and to move forward. Acceptance is power. It is grace. It is forgiveness, and it is courage. Acceptance frees us to see things as they are and pushes us to go after the things we desire. *Acceptance* is my power word for the year. I realized that I could not make peace with certain things or certain people because I had not yet fully moved through the grieving process. There are no shortcuts on this one. You have to walk through grief in order to come out on the other side.

> Acceptance helps to bring us peace; to see something as it really IS, not as we may want it to be.

Let's talk about what acceptance looks like in action. It is easy to say we need to do something, but we need to learn how to do it so we can get the healing we desire. Acceptance is directly tied to Code 1: Know Your Value. When you accept that you are valuable, that you matter, that you are worthy, then you are empowered to do anything you want. The challenge, of course, is getting to a place of acceptance, which means that you assent to the reality or what truly is.

Acceptance comes at the end of a process. The process is usually after a period of loss, trauma, or grief. And grieving has five stages, according to Elisabeth Kübler-Ross's model from her bestselling book, *On Death and Dying*:

1. **Denial:** Our first reaction is almost always denial—"This is not happening to me."
2. **Anger:** Our second reaction is "Why is this happening to me?" and we feel angry.
3. **Bargaining:** We try to negotiate our way out of our pain; we feel the loss and try to fix it.
4. **Depression:** It hits us truly and we wallow, wail, and sulk.
5. **Acceptance:** In the final stage, we accept, we come to terms, and we try to find the peace or joy in what we have left.[1]

In the almost five decades that have followed since the release of Kübler-Ross's work, psychologists have adopted and adapted the model for how our emotions are felt and addressed in all situations, not just death. It is a process. Joyce Meyer, bestselling author and one of the world's leading practical Bible teachers, says often on her TV show *Enjoying Everyday Life* that "You can't bury things that are not dead." Too many of us attempt to bury our very "alive" emotions and get what inspirational author and publisher Louise Hay calls *dis-ease*. Dis-ease means a state of unrest, discomfort within the soul, whereas actual disease is the physical manifestation of that unrest. When you live in denial or allow anger to fester, it will make you sick. I know. I have been there.

Discover How to Release Regret

One of the most difficult challenges we face is forgiving ourselves for our own wrong choices and actions. If you think forgiving others is hard, try truly forgiving you.

When I was a much younger woman I got involved in an inappropriate intimate relationship. I could make many excuses, but none of them matters. Once I realized what I had allowed myself to get involved in, I had a responsibility to get out. I confessed my secret to a fierce woman of faith, my best friend, and my mom, and they helped me to find the courage to release myself from the entanglement.

I got counseling, but shame kept me stuck for many years. I was still feeling pain, regret, and deep remorse. I never forgave myself for violating every tenet of my Code as a woman of faith and as a woman of honor.

Please do not miss the gravity of what I am sharing, because no matter what you did in your past, if it still haunts you, you have yet to make peace with it. And you must do so in order to get free.

So I did something about it: I wrote a letter that I had hand delivered. I apologized for my part in not ending the relationship sooner, and I offered forgiveness. I received a response that was very similar. We both wished each other well and apologized for the hurt we had caused. We both wanted to heal, forgive ourselves, and move forward. *And we have.*

Here is the point of sharing this story: First, it was a chapter in my life, not the whole book. Once I found the courage to turn the page, I was able to write a new, healthy chapter around loving and being loved. However, it wasn't until I decided to take action to release the remorse that I kept replaying in my mind, however, that I healed from the hurt. I made peace with what happened. I learned from it, and now I can share it openly with you and help you find the courage to release whatever is in your past.

There is a deeper point, though. When we have unhealed hurts from our childhood, we are likely to repeat the same patterns. My relationship with my father is, regrettably, not good. I have tried over the years to make it better, but the reality is some things can only be forgiven, not fixed. And as a result, I have made some bad choices in dating and loving the wrong men because I did not learn how to be loved unconditionally and properly by the first man in my life: my father. At some point, though, we cannot blame our parents for what still hurts. I had to be accountable for my choices. And it is only then that we can face ourselves and fix what ails us. So I am asking you to face your regrets or whatever remorse you feel and take the steps today to release it.

Learn How to Turn Your Pain into Purpose

You have heard the saying, "Pain has purpose." It does—if you allow it to. At the end of the day, every bad experience, bad person, and hurtful family memory is there for us to learn from. Your pain and mine is there for us to build purpose into our lives and, if we are blessed, into the lives of others. Yet many of us like to live in what I call "the 51st state": the state of denial. It's what we do to avoid pain, grief, and any kind of negative stimulus. We may believe we are coping with or actually resolving our conflicts, but we are not.

Denial leads to destruction. And from a physical wellness standpoint, creating "illusions" or not dealing with what has hurt us can cause great damage to our bodies and our emotional health. A great book I think everyone should read is *Deadly Emotions: Understand the Mind-Body-Spirit Connection That Can Heal or Destroy You*, written by Don Colbert, MD. In the book, Colbert goes through medical and psychological findings that prove that when we don't face our toxic emotions, unresolved hurts, childhood pains, anger, or wounds, our bodies suffer and we get sick. You must face what is hurt, broken, or uncomfortable in your life in order to fix it and make peace with your past.

Living the Code

Here are five steps you can take if you are struggling with your past and what has hurt you in your past:

1. **Confront the pain to get it out.** You are only as sick as your secrets. Whatever you are hiding has the potential to make you physically and emotionally unwell. If you can learn to live authentically and transparently, you will live a much longer, healthier, more prosperous life. Do not keep someone's ugly secret that they deposited in your spirit. If you were molested, abused, or hurt as a child or even as an adult, find a trustworthy person, a professional, and talk it out. Secrets can make us sick.

2. **Get professional help.** I speak of what I know. I had a lot of ailments as a child and still do as an adult. They were and are all related to stress and my immune system. Had I not gone to counseling, gone to support groups, talked it out, and used my mess as my message in life, I don't think I would be where I am today in my growth and wellness.

3. **Forgive yourself.** We suffer because we cannot forgive ourselves for what we believe we allowed someone to do to us or take from us. Forgiving yourself is critical to being able to release what has a hold on your heart.

4. **Find the courage to deal with the pain.** If you won't face what is wrong then you will never realize your full potential. Carrying baggage weighs us down. It is only when we release the baggage that we can soar to greater heights and be who we are meant to be. Fixing what is broken in your soul frees you to fly. It unleashes power in you that can change the world. Fixing you blesses the rest of us with your amazing gifts!

5. **Surround yourself with people who speak life into you.** The power of life and death is in our words. It is in our networks, our relationships, and ourselves. You heal by being affirmed and restored. Words have great power. Make sure the people surrounding you speak words that empower, bless, lift, and heal your broken, wounded places. This is so critical once we find the courage to face what ails us and dare to fix it.

🔑 Key Words

Pain	Release	Bury what is dead
Purpose	Healing	Learn the lessons
Past	Peace	
Memories	Confession	

Code
3

Teach People How
to Treat You

Be careful what you tolerate, you are teaching people how to treat you.
—Unknown

One of the most important truths I've learned in life is that we unintentionally give permission to others to mistreat us and take advantage of our goodness. But I've also learned this: People will treat you exactly how you empower them to. More importantly, they will cross boundaries we set only when we allow them the opportunity. Often we just want to keep the peace, but if we are going to live joyful, fulfilling lives, we have to stop elevating others' needs above our own. In essence, we attract more of what we allow.

We teach others how to treat us. Like it or not, it is the truth.

This truth, this Code, has been one of life's hardest lessons for me to learn. It wasn't until recently that I started to truly grasp the importance of how we give people permission to do the *right things* or the *wrong things* in our lives. I had to start looking at me. And today, I am asking you to start looking at you. I once overheard someone say, "Don't treat people how *you* want to be treated. Treat them as *they* want to be treated." People really do teach us how they want to be treated for better or worse.

Bottom line: you and I are responsible for choosing those to whom we give access to our lives. Whether or not we want to admit it, we give people the ability to help us or to hurt us. We are accountable for what we show and teach other people about us.

Every day, in ways large and small, we show people how to speak to us, work with us, and love us.

When we "teach" someone how to treat us, we give them cues, instructions about who we are, what we like, and what we expect. When this Code is out of kilter, we don't give people the right cues. This puts us in the untenable position of accepting whatever is thrown our way and settling for what we get in life versus getting what we want from life.

> If we do not know our value, we cannot teach people how to treat us with value.

Code 1 (Know Your Value) and this Code 3 are connected because they relate directly to how we value ourselves and how we teach others to value us. If we do not know our value, we cannot teach people how to treat us with value. Love, kindness, respect, empathy, honor, and peace all emanate from the same place: *a place of knowing*. When we feel worthless, we end up settling for whatever life throws our way. I know this firsthand. But I learned how to shift.

We are going to begin the journey of teaching people how to treat us as we desire by addressing three key points:

1. What your presence tells others about you
2. What you do tells others how to treat you
3. How to teach people to treat you well

People take cues from us. People watch how we value ourselves. They listen to what we say. They look to see how confident we are or are not. They watch to see how vibrant and resilient we are or are not. They quietly observe how we interact with others, and most importantly, how we treat ourselves. We send silent messages about what we value to everyone who comes into contact with us. The silent messages we send are more obvious than you think, particularly to people who have predatory instincts. Awareness is the key to making sure you surround yourself with good people who see your value, who will value you, and who will treat you well.

What Your Presence Tells Others about You

When things go wrong in our interpersonal relationships, it is always easier to blame the other person for what went wrong. But that is not a healthy way to live. The reality is that people handle us in *direct proportion* to how we have taught them to.

Before I go any further, however, let me be crystal clear about what I am NOT saying with this Code. I am not suggesting that you are in any way responsible for someone who mistreated you as a child, abused you, or made you feel worthless. You did not cause someone to sexually abuse you. You did not cause your spouse to be unfaithful to you. You did not cause your best friend to be disloyal to you. You did not teach other kids in school to call you hateful names. You did not cause your parents' divorce. You did not make your sibling envy you because you were born prettier or with more talents. You did not cause a bitter, envious colleague to steal your promotion or blackball you at the job. NO. You are not responsible for someone else's behavior.

What you are responsible for is how you respond to it, recover from it, and ultimately thrive despite it all. Once you become aware that you are not being treated as you desire, you are obligated to speak up and make a change. The truth is that you do not ever have to feel bad about removing someone from your life if they do not know how to honor you. If someone is causing you pain, discomfort, or constantly making you feel small, you need to release them. If a person continually crosses your boundaries, violates your peace, and treats you in unkind, harmful ways, they need to go.

> Once you become aware that you are not being treated as you desire, you are obligated to speak up and make a change.

The truth is, sometimes we meet bad people. Sometimes we meet broken people. They do not share our Life Code. They do not mean us well. Regardless of what you may have been told about yourself growing up or how you may have been defined in your family, you should be treated like the priceless treasure you are. I want you to start loving you. As I have had to learn to love me.

I want you with every breath you take and with every word you utter to exude confidence, self-worth, and positivity. We all have days when we don't like ourselves, when we don't feel that we are living up to the goals, dreams, and hopes we have for ourselves. That is normal. But we must never allow others to feel that we do not value ourselves, and that in turn it is somehow okay for others to not value us either. For example, we all have the woman friend who is independent, smart, attractive, and large in her presence (even if she is small in stature). She commands respect because she carries herself in such a way that she leaves no doubt that she is comfortable in her own skin and capable of doing whatever she wants to do in life. She conveys a sense of purpose that draws people to her and not from her. She is not intimidating; she is incandescent. She is not "image"; she is 100 percent authentic.

On the other hand, we all have that friend who is shy and doesn't know her power. This woman has potential, but she doesn't see her gifts, and she lacks the confidence to walk in them. When this woman walks into a room no one notices her. This woman sends a message that she is only interested in playing a supporting role. She doesn't feel beautiful, fabulous, or gifted. She feels defeated. She is every bit as intelligent and capable as the first woman, but she does not view herself, her wants, or her needs as important, and as a result she feels walked over, disrespected, passed over, or worse.

Each of these women gets back what she gives out. From the moment we show up in the world, we begin to radiate love, resilience, and possibilities in life; or we become radioactive with negativity, self-pity, and bitterness. Rarely have I met someone who doesn't fit into one of these two categories. We teach people how to treat us from the moment we first meet them. We radiate either power or powerlessness. Hence, my job in this Code, perhaps more than any other, is to help you get out of your own way and get out of the blame mode. It's normal that when life starts to hurt, we begin to look for someone to blame. We blame God, our parents, the people who broke our heart, and the people who walked away. We lament because we didn't get the loan or we got fired unfairly. Whatever it is that we think we lost we invariably link back to it as the source of our pain. *I get it. I have done it.* But we always have the choice to take the defeats of our lives and turn them into dreams. Anytime we wake up unhappy with life we have a choice to say, "This is not how my story will end."

> Anytime we wake up unhappy with life we have a choice to say, "This is not how my story will end."

We love to point the finger at everyone but us. It is hard to look at yourself and say, "I let him treat me like that." Or "I allowed her to cross my professional boundaries." Or "She was never really my friend." The problem is that we don't ask the deeper questions: "Why did I allow this?" Or "When did I start giving people permission to do the wrong things in my life?" You and I decide who gets access to our lives. We must also be willing to accept ownership for our part in what happens when we end up discarded, disrespected, or worse. We all know what it feels like to have that *aha* moment when you have to own the fact that you let someone mistreat you. You saw the red flags. But you ignored them. Why? Because you do not believe you are worthy of love. It is that simple.

What You Do Tells Others How to Treat You

If you are always running yourself ragged and speaking poorly about yourself, others will run you ragged and speak poorly about you too. If you are a pessimist who never sees the good in life, people will not want to be around you. If you push good people away and punish them for the wrongs others have done to you, good people will stop coming your way. If you always have to be the hero (or *shero*) in the story, if you act as if you wear a big *S* on your chest and that you can leap tall buildings in a single bound, then people will treat you like Superwoman. And they will not be there when you need to be rescued.

Let me pause here. One of the most dangerous things any woman can do is to give the impression that she is never in need, always in control, and never vulnerable. Part of how we teach people to treat us is when we show them that we never need help. That we never cry. That we will always figure a way out on our own. If this is you, I need you to STOP. Right now: STOP. *Superwoman syndrome* is probably the number one *dis-ease* among women today. Our mothers and grandmothers knew how to rest. They knew how to get still. To be silent. To embrace other women and fellowship with them. We have lost the art of intimacy and connection. And in doing so, we have built up the false impression that we are always okay. And the truth is, *we are not.*

We set ourselves up for failure. We take on these impossible roles and we teach people that we have no boundaries. We teach people that they can dump on us, use us, and then forget us. We teach the people closest to us that they matter but we do not. We wonder why no one comes to take care of us. We are in our own way. We block our blessings and deepest desires from becoming reality because we keep repeating the negative things we were taught about our value. We have to stop.

> If you set boundaries with your family, your friends, and on your job, you will be a much happier person.

If you set boundaries with your family, your friends, and on your job, you will be a much happier person. If you are a single professional woman, stop volunteering to stay late for work. Stop working on weekends and holidays. If you are always showing people that you don't have a life outside of work, do not get mad when they treat you that way.

I have not always taught the people in my life to treat me very well. This is something I have just recently admitted after years of counseling and attending Al-Anon meetings. As I mentioned in Code 1, knowing your value starts in your family. And in my family I was always defined as strong, successful, and reliable. But my best title was *fixer*.

I learned early on in my life not to need much emotionally, to be very independent, and never to cry, because tears flowed too often in my home amidst the screams, fighting, and cursing coming from a drunken and oftentimes mean father. My frightened mother and younger brother would often cower in a corner. And me, well, I would push back. But I internalized a lot of unhealthy, damaging behaviors, and I learned to bury my feelings and smile. My "boundaries" light was badly dimmed for a long time. I learned to accept as normal behavior that which was completely abnormal—particularly for a Christian household, because who we said we were at church was not at all who we were behind closed doors.

Here's the point of my sharing this history: *The Code of my family for generations* was rancor, violence, anger, eruptions, disrespectful language, hiding emotions, and verbally abusing others one day, and the next day pretending it did not happen. I lived like this for my first eighteen years. Until one day I made a decision that I would no longer be party to such dishonesty and deception. When I got to college, I got help, because if I had kids, I didn't want them to grow up like me. I wanted to break the generational curse that was so clearly upon my family. Unfortunately, we can only work on ourselves and do the best we can to heal from the negative things we saw growing up.

And some members of my family have punished me for it. They still do. All because I refuse to be treated in ways that violate me as a human being and as a woman of faith, and I stand up for myself. People who want to remain in their dysfunction will never appreciate you getting out of yours. Misery indeed loves company.

Moreover, I am happy to say that I have begun to make the hard decisions and that I have found the strength to love myself enough to remove anyone from my life who cannot see my value, honor my Code, and treat me with the love and respect with which I do my best every day to treat others.

I'm sharing my story because somebody out there reading this book right now doesn't know how to get past the pain of her upbringing. Code 2 (Make Peace with Your Past) outlines how to start. *But it is a journey.* You just have to know your value and dare to demand more for yourself. People will respond to what you tolerate or not. Your goal has to be to stop operating in the same dysfunction and the same unhealthy patterns that have enabled people to mistreat you.

Here's the thing, ladies: all change starts with you and with me. I had to begin to take ownership of who I was surrounding myself with and why. I had to look at some of my most intimate relationships and make hard decisions (even within my immediate family) about who was toxic and who needed to go. I am becoming very protective of my sacred space, which Dr. Maya Angelou taught us was so important. I don't want negative energy in my space. Life is just too short. My point: the journey to teaching people how to treat us in the ways we most desire and most need begins within.

How to Teach People to Treat You Well

If you find yourself unhappy with how you are being treated, if you feel you are always being taken for granted, used, or even abused by people in your life, it's time for you to do a *self-check*. I did one, and I discovered that, on the whole, I have amazingly positive, wonderful, loving, supportive, good people in my life. They challenge me, chasten me, correct me, adore me, build me, give to me, and they are as loyal to me as I am to them. *Do not miss this*. We are alike. So we don't fuss, fight, or have drama because we operate by a similar Code of integrity, temperament, loyalty, and relationship.

When I looked back at some of the relationships that made me feel mishandled in my career or abused emotionally by loved ones, I found a common thread:

- If anyone in my *family* felt they could treat me badly based on our family history of dysfunction, denial, and cover-up, they were doing what had always been done.

- In a *dating or romantic relationship*, I always ended up dating my father in some form or fashion—handsome, withdrawn, controlling, emotionally unavailable men who had mommy issues and who were outwardly successful but inwardly damaged.

- If *women I befriended* tended to be overly aggressive, kind of mean girl (even abrasive with glee) alpha chicks, they did not share my value system, my faith system, or my Code of conduct system.

"Likes," as my Nana used to say, "last." I realize that I value myself; I want to honor myself; I am strong, successful, kind, good, loving, and caring because those are the kinds of people I have in my inner circle, in my "front row" (see Code 17). Those are the people I have attracted into my life. They will do anything for me. They know how to appreciate the "gift of me" as I appreciate the gift of them.

Living the Code

Here are five strategies that will help you attract positive, loving, stable people. If you incorporate them into your life, you will begin to experience a freedom and self-confidence you never knew existed.

1. **Set boundaries.** If you don't have healthy boundaries, if you don't rest, if you don't take care of yourself, people will take advantage of you. You have to let people know that you honor yourself and that those who cause drama or seek to drain you will be removed quickly.

2. **Understand your Life Code.** What matters to you? Loyalty, integrity, reciprocity, laughter? Whatever it is, find that in other people. Attract like-minded people who share your Code. If you fool around with people who do not value what you value, your life will be drama-filled.

3. **Know how people resolve conflict.** I like to TALK things out. No matter how uncomfortable or challenging, at some point mature adults have to talk and seek to resolve things in ways that make us better, wiser people. Do not suffer people who hurt you and then leave you to clean up their mess. Find out how people resolve conflicts before you get attached to or work with them, because all human relationships have conflict.

4. **Surround yourself with people who speak your "love language."** I am a gift giver, a letter writer, an expressive person. And I will give my time, network, and access pretty freely. I value those things being poured back into me. The relationships that thrive make me feel secure and valued, and they speak my language. It is reflex for my inner circle to support me and love me because they are like me.

5. **Let your faith guide how you treat others.** I am a practicing Christian. Do I have some issues? *You bet I do.* I can be short-tempered if I feel misused or taken for granted. On the other hand, my natural personality is engaging, easygoing, and very kindhearted. I give to a fault, and my love of God drives the woman *I try to be* every day. My faith is my Life Code, and it tells me it matters how we treat people and how we allow them to treat us.

In the final analysis, we teach people what we will tolerate from them. Get quiet and ask yourself how you are teaching people to treat you. It is the most important question you can ever ask yourself. Do it today. Then make a plan to release anyone or anything that does not honor the priceless, precious gift of you.

Key Words

Teach	Spirit	Exude
Treat you	Ethics	Value
Code	Self-Check	
Blame	Command	

Live Authentically

> Authenticity is a collection of choices that we have to make every day. It's about the choice to show up and be real. The choice to be honest. The choice to let out true selves be seen.
>
> —Brené Brown

Being "authentic" sounds good, but what does it really mean? In simplest terms, it means to be yourself. But being your true self is never easy, particularly in a world obsessed with celebrity, good looks, Snapchat, TikTok videos, and perfect lives captured in beautiful photographs posted all over social media. Only none of that has anything to do with reality. Authenticity is all about being you when *everyone* else is looking. Being authentic is all about loving yourself, liking yourself, and knowing your value.

To be who we are truly meant to be is no easy thing, especially in a world that values what is fake, what is easy, what is quick, and what is on the surface.

Part of your Code—and mine—is authenticity. This is the purest and most valuable part of who we are. It is also the most quickly abandoned. The first sign of abandoning this Code happens when we are teenage girls turning into women. By the time we become teenagers, we have been stripped of our inner Code, and we want to fit in, we want to belong, so we become cheerleaders, join sororities, hitch our wagons closely to other young women we so desperately want to be like. This is our shared plight as women, the struggle to be independent yet interdependent, the need to be an individual but also part of the crowd.

Women face immense pressure to conform. We are bombarded with ads and images that tell us who we should be as girls and who we should become as women. These campaigns stress what is *external* versus what is *internal*. They tell us that we are nothing unless we are attractive, thin, and sexy. Let me be clear: being an authentic woman has absolutely nothing to do with any of those things.

Look, I get that part of our Code is to care about how others see us. "Image" and self-image have great power for us and in our culture. Despite all our amazing gains in the sciences, the arts, academia, medicine, politics, and entertainment, we women still allow ourselves to be defined by our body image, how others see us, and our ability to take care of others.

> This is our shared plight as women, the struggle to be independent yet interdependent, the need to be an individual but also part of the crowd.

The notion of "image" starts with definitions, and those definitions are often not our own. Over time, we may find ourselves falling in line with societal norms, family expectations, the traps of our own poor choices, or the desires others have for us. Yet women are starting to push back. We do want it all, but we don't want the weight of the weariness, stress, pressure, sacrifice, and *dis-ease* that come with trying to have it all. Something inside us says this is not the way life is supposed to be lived. *There is a way for me to live up to all I am gifted to be and not lose myself in the process.* Let's face it, Sisters of the Code, the rules are still different for us.

In this Code, we will focus on three keys to help you unlock the authentic you.

1. Define what it means to be authentic.
2. Recognize and remove the enemies of authenticity.
3. Create an authentic life.

Living authentically is never easy, but it is very rewarding. Life is so fragile and we are here for such a short time. We have so many gifts to give the world, but far too many of us have hidden our gifts not only from the world, but most importantly from ourselves. We spend our lives "hiding" our true selves in order to dance to someone else's music. It is time for us to learn to live out the power of authenticity.

Define What It Means to Be Authentic

To be authentic is to be an original. It is to be true and not false. It is to be pure, rare, and verifiable. When we learn to unlock the Code of "original," of "reliable," of "trustworthy," and of "self," we are living an authentic life. To be authentic, then, means learning to be yourself. And as ironic as it may seem, being yourself can be difficult when your Code has been rewritten to meet someone else's vision of your life.

A great place to start practicing the art of being authentic is in defining what it means to you to be authentically you. To be authentic is to discover. It is to create. It is to refresh. It is to dance. It is to soar. You must have self-awareness in order to know who you are and what you want from life. "Authenticity is about being genuine and real," says Mike Robbins, a former major league baseball player, a corporate trainer, and the author of *Be Yourself, Everyone Else Is Already Taken.* Authenticity allows us to connect deeply with others because it requires us to be transparent and vulnerable. "It is important because it liberates us from the pressures of always trying to be something else, always trying to be perfect," Robbins says.[1] Authenticity starts when you set the intention to be genuine. Then, there must be an awareness of what that looks and feels like and a willingness to act

> To be authentic is to discover. It is to create. It is to refresh. It is to dance. It is to soar.

in accordance with your genuine nature even when being genuine feels vulnerable.

When you live in the sacred space of self-awareness, life becomes easier because you are free to choose things that most closely mirror your values and your Code. To be authentic is to stand in a place of total acceptance of yourself. It frees you to thrive versus just exist. But there is a downside: being authentic means you must be willing to go against the crowd. Authenticity requires that you make unpopular decisions. And it requires that you be willing to show your complete self to the world. Authenticity leads to honesty and openness with the people in your life and the people you want to attract into your life.

And there is more good news: when we dare to live authentically, we are physically and emotionally healthier. According to research (similar to what you will read in Code 6, Guard Your Heart), when you are true to your dreams, your hopes, and yourself, you improve your relationships, your health, and your overall wellness. "Authentic people feel better," according to researchers Michael Kernis and Brian Goldman. In a 2002 article, "The Role of Authenticity in Healthy Psychological Functioning and Subjective Well-Being," published in the *Annals of the American Psychotherapy Association*,[2] Kernis and Goldman say they found that people who understand the power of authenticity are:

- More resilient
- Less likely to turn to drugs, alcohol, or addictive habits as coping mechanisms in difficulty
- More likely to be purposeful and focused in their life goals
- More likely to follow through on their goals

On the other hand, people who are not living authentically are more likely to experience these emotions:

- Feeling fragmented or broken apart
- Feeling unhappy

- Feeling bored, stuck, or otherwise uninspired
- Feeling pulled by life instead of having the power to PUSH life as they want it to go

Recognize and Remove the Enemies of Authenticity

Now that we have a working definition of what it means to be authentic, let's talk about how we can spot and remove those people, places, or things that distract us and keep us from becoming authentic. Distraction is the enemy of focus. And being authentic requires self-focus. A distraction is a "thing" that keeps you from giving your full attention to something or someone of importance and value.

Regardless of our age, geographical location, or social status, we are very easily distracted. We have the distractions of work, family, career, marriage, friendships, school, exercise, routines, and charitable demands. We have 24/7 lives now; we feel we are always on call. Hence, it is easy to get lost. And it is easy to lose your authentic self in the hustle and bustle of it all. Here are five ways you can recognize what is causing you to live your life on other people's terms:

1. You never take time out for you. You don't even know who you are or what you have to offer in life. This tends to be a big issue in midlife.
2. You never consider what you want or what you need from life and those in your life. You never ask for what you need. Instead, you shrink back. You remain silent. And you suffer.
3. You are still living up to your parents' goals and dreams long after you have become a mature adult.
4. You are covering up unresolved pain that weighs you down. You want out but you don't know how to get out from under the heaviness, depression, and guilt.

5. You are in a job or marriage or relationship you hate and that does not honor you, and yet you stay out of fear of the unknown.

These five areas are huge distracters. Your inability to take time out for you is the biggest distraction you will face as a woman. By not taking time out to get to know you, you allow the greedy monster of "busy" to overtake you. You are always exhausted, weary, and stressed out. You say you will make time for you, but you never do. And the years fly by, the decades turn, and you are stuck wishing for a different life but never daring to make it so.

Worse, you never ask for what you need from those who depend upon you. And it leaves you feeling quietly resentful. Perhaps you are in a job or career path that does not line up with your passions and purpose. You trudge along and you do what must be done, but inside you are slowly dying. You are screaming for help. You want to be rescued. In reality the hero, the rescuer, in your story is you. Only you can make the changes that free you from the distractions that keep you stuck and wanting so much more.

Create an Authentic Life

Our world is very different from the worlds our mothers, grand-mothers, and great-grandmothers inhabited. They lived a certain way because they had few rights and few choices. They had little time to spend dreaming and creating authentic lives. We are their heirs. And we have something they did not: *the power of choice.*

True power has nothing to do with what you own, what your title is at work, or how much money you have in the bank. True power is answering your call in life. It is daring not only to be au-thentic with yourself but to live authentically with others. We are on a quest for balance and life integration that helps us and does not hinder us. We don't just want to collect a paycheck; we want purpose. We crave connection with others on an intimate level

versus *hello, how are you, let's get together sometime*. We want
to know our family history, connect with aging family members,
and really get to know our siblings and parents.

Bottom line: we want authenticity in all that we do and in all
that we touch. We are restless and tired because we are stuck in
routines and in comfort zones that don't truly move us. We want
something to look forward to, something to keep us on our toes in
life. Take a look around you, Sisters of the Code. There is a spiritual awakening going on—from Oprah's *Super Soul Sunday*, to
the explosive growth of megachurches, to the Hallmark Channel
movies that focus on our spirit and in finding the hero that resides
within. Spiritually speaking, we no longer wish to just do church.
We are looking for that which resonates in our souls. We want God
at his essence, we want love at its essence, we want friendship at its
essence, and we want life at its essence. So how do we create that
life? It starts by being willing to redefine for ourselves what success means, moving away from traditional standards of what work
means, what love means, and what living life means. The shift has
to occur in our hearts first. Being authentic occurs in your heart.
And once you wake up to who you really are and to who you are
capable of being, life will never be the same.

Creating an authentic life that makes you happy starts inside. I
speak from experience. I was thirty-eight years old, sitting in my
law office in Washington, DC, preparing to become a partner the
following year, when I started to experience chest pains. I went to
GW Hospital across the street, and a team of doctors ran tests. I
was on the fast track. I was dating a very eligible man with a great
job at Deloitte. We were a "handsome" couple, as the old folks like
to say. We fit. We would make pretty babies, have a big house in
the suburbs of Virginia, and live happily ever after. Right? Wrong.

I did not love him. In fact, I am not even sure I liked him. He
just fit the script. Yet life has a funny way of giving us a chance to
escape the impending prisons we set for ourselves. My heart wasn't

the problem; instead I got an unexpected diagnosis. I was told that as a result I would never have children, and, long story short, he walked away. The irony is, the doctors got it wrong.

But the lessons that came from that very difficult period in my life were immense. I needed to see who was authentic in my life. I'll never forget the dozens of women friends who prayed with me and over me. I'll never forget the awakening that took place in my life just a year later when I finally admitted to myself that I hated being an attorney and that I did not want to be a partner in a big law firm. I'll never forget the huge release of stress I felt when I told my family and friends that I was going to pursue my deep desire to become a writer and journalist. They all thought I was nuts. Maybe I was nuts. But looking back now, eight years later, I know that I was 100 percent right.

I didn't marry that man, who on the surface looked so right for me. And I still do not have the children I so deeply desired. However, I did become an award-winning freelance journalist for major newspapers and magazines and, best of all, an award-winning author with my second book now in your hands. My point in sharing this story is to say this: I was headed down a dismal road of conformity, expectations to be fulfilled, and an existence that would have swallowed me whole. I was never meant to live someone else's vision of my life, and neither are you. If I can change my life, so can you!

So how do you create a life of authenticity? You create it as I did. You wake up one day and you have a courageous conversation (see Code 19) with yourself. You stop making what your family thinks, what your spouse thinks, what your friends think, or what the world demands more important than what *you* think. You wake up one day and you say, "Enough. I am going to live my life for me before it is over." You make a deal with yourself to release what no longer serves you. To get rid of that which hinders you. To grasp that it is never too late to have a life and never too late to change one. You don't need to be rescued. You need only to be awakened.

I promise you, Sisters of the Code, when you dare to have a real, authentic conversation with yourself, all will be well. Not only will it be well, but you will rediscover who you are. The real you. The you the world wants to get to know.

Living the Code

Being authentic is first cousin to knowing your value. And of all the Codes in this book, Know Your Value and Live Authentically are the most critical to your well-being and success. If you know your value, you will embrace your gifts and you will walk in authenticity.

Here are several things I have put into practice in my own life, some of which I have adapted from "self-help" gurus. Put them into practice in your own life and watch what happens.

1. **Know your value.** I will keep repeating this Code over and over until you catch on. Everything we do as women starts with this.

2. **Face your inner demons.** You cannot live an authentic life with a bunch of mess swirling around in your head. You have to do the work. "Stuff" covers up our "source Code." You have to de-clutter to get to who you are inside. Being authentic is all about removing the junk other people have pushed on us and around us.

3. **Ask the hard questions.** Ask the people around you who get you, love you, and are there for you what they see in you. Sometimes we don't see what others can. Ask for help in finding your purpose. And mostly, get still and quiet with you so that you can hear the answers from within.

4. **Dare to redefine.** I don't care if you are twenty or sixty, it is never too late to be who you might have been. But you cannot

get there if you don't have the courage to make changes. Being authentic is all about being flexible with yourself.

5. **Trust your instincts.** Of all I have learned in my forty-something years of living, among the most important is that I need to trust my intuition and instinct. That is your authentic self talking to your false self. You need to listen to that voice inside of you and follow.

6. **Connect with people who share your Code.** This is big, Sisters. You have to run with other "authentic" people. Period. If you spend time with shallow, surface, masked people, you will become one. Surround yourself with people who are transparent, honest, and authentic.

⚷ Key Words

Authentic	Create	Trust
Transparent	Reveal	Redefine
Real	Self	Value
Honest	Clarity	Awareness
Original	Courage	
Evolved	Dreams	

Section II

The Emotional Codes

Our emotions as women are at times both a blessing and a curse. These four Codes will help women to recognize and better manage their emotions from a place of wisdom, self-reflection, self-love, and resilience.

Code 5

Be Accountable for Your Life

At the end of the day we are accountable to ourselves—our success is a result of what we do.

—Catherine Pulsifer

Y ou want to clear a room real fast? Start talking about being accountable. Nobody likes the word "accountability." Maybe it's because being accountable means we must do a daily self-check. We must self-correct, not just in our personal and emotional lives, but in our professional lives, too. None of us like to be wrong. We have to consider our actions and their impact not just on others, but most of all on ourselves, each and every day of our lives. Success in life is directly tied to humility and our ability to own our faults, admit our mistakes, and have the courage to change and be better.

Let's face it, we live in a culture that rejects the notion of personal accountability. We see it everywhere. We don't want to own our choices or our decisions. We lament: *It's my parents' fault; it's my ex's fault; it's the high school cheerleading coach's fault; it's the college admission director's fault; it's my abuser's fault; it's the boss's fault; it's society's fault;* and grandest of all, *it's the church's fault!* And when we have a disagreement or conflict with the women in our lives, we say, *It was all her fault!*

We love to play the blame game. We want to point to everybody's faults and shortcomings but our own. We do not want to do the hard work required to own our behavior. This is unfortunate, because the only way we grow is by learning from our mistakes and poor choices. Being woman enough to handle these mistakes and choices with grace and wisdom is the challenge.

I read a quote from Bishop Tudor Bismark on Twitter recently that I will never forget: "What you refuse to be ACCOUNTABLE for will become your MASTER, then it will RULE you, and then it will DESTROY you." His point is simple: What you will not deal with will deal with you. What you refuse to apologize for, be responsible for, make change for, and own will ultimately be the thing that destroys you.

Before I go further, let me make a disclaimer: some of what hurts in your life right now may well be someone else's fault. I empathize, trust me. I am not mocking or making fun. There is no deeper wound than to be injured by others and then have them not take responsibility for the injury and leave us holding the bag.

The hurt can eat you alive! We spend years lamenting that person's lack of accountability for the injury. We wonder how someone can injure another, then walk away without so much as a second thought about his or her own behavior! There is no answer to such a question. All I can tell you is what I tell myself: You are not responsible for what someone else did to you as a child or young adult. You cannot govern other people's behavior. Your job (and mine) as an adult is to make sure you are healed, whole, and happy. Please know that I am not saying people should be let off the hook for what they have done to your life. What I am saying is that the only person's conduct you can govern is your own. Period. What I am learning (slowly) is that when I focus on my life, my Code, my words, my thoughts, and my actions, I actually turn out to be a much happier, peaceful, and more connected human being.

As we discussed in Code 2 (Make Peace with Your Past), you have to release the things you cannot change. They are done. They are behind you. You cannot fix what someone else broke. But you can fix you. You can be accountable to you. You can find the courage to look yourself in the eye and say this is not how my story is going to end. In this Code we are going to take a hard look at SELF. There can be no greater challenge than the challenge to conquer self. To do so requires that we take our eyes off those who may have hurt us and dare to look inward and develop a Code of conduct that says, "No matter what others may or may not do, I will be accountable for my actions, my choices, my words, and my needs."

I am asking you to be courageous. Personal accountability starts with the ability to take an honest look at who we are and where we are. Hiding serves nothing and no one. Denial is only a delay of the inevitable. If you want to be a good person with great relationships and a meaningful life, then it starts with how you are accountable to your Code. In this Code we will break down three keys of accountability:

1. Learn what accountability is.
2. Realize that accountability matters.
3. Create a life of personal accountability.

Learn What Accountability Is

To account for something is simply to explain what you have done, what you see, what you feel, what you need, what you think, or to acknowledge what remains after an event or experience. Being accountable for your actions, thoughts, goals, and dreams is to be *responsible* for them, to understand them, and to take ownership of them. Be willing to improve them, and to learn from them. To be accountable is to take stock, to be engaged in, and to take control of your life.

Taking ownership of your life is the single most important ingredient to becoming a successful person. You will never find a successful person who makes excuses, dodges personal responsibility, or blames others for what is not working in their life. Successful people are go-getters. They also understand the immense power of answering not just to one's self but to others with whom they are in relationship (whether in love, business, friendship, or fellowship). They surround themselves with truth tellers and people who will hold them to account so that they can grow wiser, richer, faster, and stronger. Accountability begins with a goal. For example, when you're in high school, you set a goal to become a physician. You *accept* that you will have to do something to become a doctor. You will need to get good grades in college and get accepted into medical school. You will need to give up years of your young adult life to working toward this goal. You will not get to attend all the parties and be with your friends. Your path will require discipline, determination, and many nights of study.

If, however, along the way you decide to backpack in Europe or "find yourself," then wake up at thirty-five and find you have not yet become a doctor, you can only look at you. You will have made choices that have predictable consequences.

Second, "personal accountability" encompasses ALL phases of your life process—*the before, during, and after*. You must be WILLING (not forced) to PERSONALLY take ownership for all you do. As I noted earlier, the word *acceptance* is key here because when we take ownership for our actions and choices in life, we are making a pact with ourselves to be okay with what we do, how we do it, and whatever consequences (good or bad) follow. That is why successful people thrive in life. They make a decision (which is another critical element of personal accountability) to be okay with their choices. And they move forward always learning, growing, and accepting the outcomes of those choices.

Accountability, then, is

- Understanding and accepting who you are and what you value;
- Putting behind you those people, places, and things that can serve as negative distractions, idols, or excuses in your life;

- Taking actions to live out those values (Code); and
- Answering for the results, regardless of the outcome to yourself and others.

Only after we make a decision to be accountable can we unlock the amazing, vibrant life waiting inside that longs once and for all to be free from excuses, blame, and denial. When you make the decision to own your life, to own your story, you are empowering yourself to win.

Realize That Accountability Matters

You are responsible for your life. This is the principle you must embrace if you plan for happiness and success in your relationships and in your work. When we allow ourselves to be accountable, we are making a decision to live life authentically for all to see. As inspirational author Brené Brown said during *Oprah's Lifeclass*, which aired in September 2013, "Authenticity is a collection of choices that we have to make every day. It's about the choice to show up and be real. The choice to be honest. The choice to let our true selves be seen."

To me, this is what accountability is all about and why it matters so much to our lives. When you allow the people you work with, love, and lead to know that you are accountable and that they are free to hold you accountable, it frees them to be authentic, vulnerable, and real. It creates a safe space, a place of honesty and comfort. There is nothing more detrimental to a relationship than for the people involved to feel

> When you allow the people you work with, love, and lead to know that you are accountable and that they are free to hold you accountable, it frees them to be authentic, vulnerable, and real. It creates a safe space, a place of honesty and comfort.

that they are unable to ask questions, be heard, and feel protected and honored by those they love and trust.

Sandra and Stephanie are lifelong friends. They have known each other since grade school. After high school and college they moved to different cities, married, and started their families. They reconnected after ten years and decided to go into business together. The challenge for them began when they realized they were no longer the same people they once were. They had both grown; they were no longer the two girls who shared pigtails and braces. Friction started between them, and they were fighting all the time. Stephanie, the accountant, handled the financial end of the business. She called me for some personal coaching, and I came up with a set of principles (or what I call an accountability grid) that each woman agreed to honor so they could get past their styles and their ten-year gap of life experiences to get in touch with their shared "Code."

Here is their accountability grid:

- They had to agree that they had financial and legal accountability to one another as business partners.
- They had to agree they had a moral and relational accountability to each other as lifelong friends who had been separated for a time but who still loved and respected one another greatly.
- They had to agree that it was worth it to both of them to do the hard work to be accountable, have courageous conversations (see Code 19), and to do so with the end result of building a successful business.

Once I got them to agree to the basic "Code" (because true connection with other people can only come when people feel heard, valued, loved, and mutually honored), then we got down to why it benefited them to be accountable to their shared goals and to each other. When we agree to be accountable first to self, then to others, our relationships deepen and thrive beyond our wildest imaginations. Here are just a few reasons why being accountable matters:

- **It reduces stress/depression/arguments:** Personal accountability allows us to start and complete actions that we know need to be done. It allows us to follow and live out our dreams and avoid the guilt and stress of not doing so. When we are accountable we can own our part like adults who want to change and grow for the better. This alleviates a lot of conflict in our lives.

- **It allows you to build trust, loyalty, and reliance on others:** By bringing accountability partners into our lives (Know Your Front Row, Code 17), we protect ourselves from ourselves. The Bible calls it "iron sharpening iron." We agree to be checked, corrected, and held to account when we stray from our purpose, or our Code.

- **It allows you to focus on what is important:** Distractions are a huge problem. Having accountability partners brings third party objectivity to a situation and sharpens our focus. When we are focused we are more likely to recognize distractions that threaten the very things we want.

- **It allows us to be attentive to our own needs and those of others:** When we are focused, and when we have a circle of trust and accountability in our lives, we are free to be attentive to the needs of others. We are free to be attentive to the needs of our heart.

The *downside* of being accountable to yourself, allowing others to hold you accountable, and holding others to account is this: it's *tough* to do. Opening yourself up (being vulnerable) to explain your actions to another person requires humility. Most of us could use a good old-fashioned life course in what it means to walk a life of humility. In its purest form, humility is "the act or posture of lowering one's self in relation to others, or conversely, having a clear perspective, and therefore respect, for one's place in context."[1]

Bottom line: being willing and able to take direction or correction from someone else is difficult. Likewise, realizing that you are not always your own "best boss," "best organizer," or "best counsellor" is hard to admit. But when you can admit that accountability is a two-way street, you are making a decision to allow others to help you to lead the life you so desperately want to live.

Create a Life of Personal Accountability

No one can live your life for you. No matter how hard you try to blame others for the events of your life, once you reach adulthood each event and its consequences are the result of choices you made and are making. Here are three practices I have incorporated into my life over the past decade and some things my mentors have taught me about using the Code of accountability to advance my life in the direction I want.

1. **Listen to the little voice in your soul.** Is that voice strong, confident, and courageous? Do you hear yourself taking responsibility, or placing blame when confronted with conflict or life storms? Learn to get still and hear that voice. It will lead you away from blame and eliminate excuses. If you notice that the blame track or the excuse track seems to play repeatedly in your mind, you are shifting responsibility for your decisions and life to others. You have to change the track. You have to take control of your present and your future. Use the past only as a guidepost by which to learn.

2. **Listen to yourself when you speak.** In your public conversation, interpersonal relationships, or management style, do you hear yourself blame others for things that don't go exactly as you want? Do you find yourself pointing fingers at your coworkers, your upbringing, your parents' influence, the amount of money you make, or your spouse? Are you making excuses for goals unmet or tasks that missed their deadlines? If you can hear your blaming patterns, you can stop them. And you can rewrite the Code that has been corrupted by your past.

3. **Don't be defensive.** If your trusted row of advisers offers you the constructive feedback that you often make excuses and

blame others for your woes, take their feedback seriously. "Wounds from a friend can be trusted, but an enemy multiplies kisses."[2] Control your natural defensive reactions and dare to explore their observations and deepen your understanding. People who responsibly consider feedback attract much more feedback. And they learn and grow.

Living the Code

Sisters of the Code, in the final analysis we can all agree that taking charge of your life starts with a decision to be held accountable. As we covered in this Code, we need to implement various kinds of accountability into our lives. According to the bestselling author of *Little Things Matter*, W. Todd Smith, there are three areas of accountability.

Area 1: Your actions and choices:

- The way in which you communicate with others
- How you spend your time
- Your behavior and manners
- The consideration and respect you show others
- Your eating habits and exercising routine
- Your attitude and thoughts
- The way you respond to challenges

Area 2: Your responsibilities:

- Returning calls, emails, and texts in a timely manner
- Being on time for business and personal appointments

- Keeping your home, car, and workplace clean
- Spending less than you earn
- Doing the things you agreed to do when you agreed to do them
- Executing your job description to the best of your ability
- Writing things down on a "To Do" list so you don't forget

Area 3: Your goals:

- Fitness and health targets
- Financial goals
- Family objectives
- Career ambitions
- Personal goals
- Marital enhancement
- Any other goals you have set for yourself[3]

You cannot achieve anything worthwhile personally or professionally if you don't hold yourself accountable. The reason is simple. It's your life! It's your journey. And at the end of the day, it's your Code. So honor it. Embrace your story. Embrace your decisions when they are good and learn from them when they are bad. In doing so you unlock your life to achieve greater heights and greater possibilities than you could ever imagine.

Key Words

Accountability	Goals	Ambitions
Decisions	Dreams	Process
Responsibility	Values	Respect
Choices	Code	Honor
Vulnerability	Consideration	Your Story

Code
6

Guard Your Heart

Guard your heart, mind and time. Those three things will determine
the health of everything else in your life.

—Andrena Sawyer

The Bible tells us to "guard your heart, for it is a wellspring of
life." We would be wise to follow this command. Women are a
mixture of power and purpose, strength and profound vulnerability.
We are kind, compassionate, empathetic. Although professionally
accomplished, we are still women—and that is special. We have
the ability to bring forth life from our bodies and love from our
hearts. When we care, we care deeply. And when we love, we love
deeply. That can be both a blessing and a curse.

We love to love. In many ways we are obsessed by it. Love has
been written about since the beginning of time, from King Solomon's poetic love verses in Scripture to the great eighteenth-century
romantic poet Lord Byron. We love a good love story. We love to
have our heartstrings tugged. Women in particular flock to romantic movies and romance novels as a form of escape in a world rife
with too much practicality, disconnection, and busyness. We long
to be still and get lost in our secret place: our heart. Because our
heart is the soul of where we live. It is the essence of what keeps
us living. It keeps us connected to others and wanting desperately
for them to stay connected to us.

We have two distinct hearts: our emotional heart and our physical heart. We often take care of the one and neglect the other. We

obsess about healthy foods, cardio workouts, and checkups. We do everything we can to keep our physical hearts healthy. But in order to be truly healthy and truly alive, we must do more than just tend to our physical heart health. We also must tend to our emotional heart health.

Being alive is more than physical. Being alive means being passionate, purposeful, loving and receiving love, and being completely engaged in life. Sadly, women have embraced technology, texting, and relationships that do not nourish our souls deeply. We settle for shallow. We build walls and keep people out. We've succumbed to a culture of "surface." We have allowed our sacred selves to be diminished by a world engrossed in selfishness. In this Code, I want to talk about what it means to harness the power of your heart to unlock your most connected, most passionate, most authentic life. This Code has major consequences if we do not get it right.

> Being alive is more than physical. Being alive means being passionate, purposeful, loving and receiving love, and being completely engaged in life.

Guarding your heart does not mean placing chains on it, starving it, withholding it, or gating it. Your heart must be protected, but it must also be honored. There are three ways to unlock the fullness of your heart:

1. Guard it; don't gate it.
2. Love people who will love you back.
3. Realize that rejection is often life's protection.

The human heart is at the epicenter of our being. It is our essence. It establishes who we are, how we feel, what we desire, whom we love, how we give, to whom we give, how we forgive, why we forgive, what we hold, and what we release. So the more quickly you learn how to give your heart to the right people and guard it from the wrong people, the better off you will be.

Guard It; Don't Gate It

The Word tells us to guard our heart because it is the "wellspring of life."[1] A wellspring is a source of a continual or abundant supply. So to have a wellspring of life inside of you is to have an abundance or inexhaustible supply of hope, love, light, energy, health, and peace. What a powerful metaphor for living—to be a well of promise, abundance, energy, and light. We all know people who possess such overflow and we all love to be near them. In 2 Corinthians 7:9–11 the apostle Paul writes about how sorrow can work *for our good or for our bad*. Sorrow can teach us. It can make us grow up and bless us.

But there is a darkness that can fall upon us, an ache, and a loneliness that can break us and lead us to death, if not a literal death, most certainly an emotional one. It can result in a heart attack, a stroke, ulcers, deep depression, or worse. Being afraid of being wounded ultimately causes us to forfeit the capacity to love. The enemy (also known as fear) would like nothing better than for us to isolate ourselves remaining chained to our doubts. "Guard your heart" becomes a means of defending ourselves from the possibility of being hurt or making mistakes in relationships.

It can also be a way of controlling our situations instead of trusting God to protect us. Guarding one's heart should not equal insulating it securely against the world. When fear is our motivator, we will become stingy with our empathy and love. We begin to rob others of the richness of who we are, and worst of all, we rob ourselves of the love we so desperately desire.

Guarding your heart is all about your Code. You protect your heart by knowing your value. You protect your heart by teaching people how to treat you. You protect your heart by knowing when to cut someone off or to *untie for a season* (see Code 12). You protect your heart by building a loyal group of friends. You protect your heart by taking care of your needs. Scripture as well as modern medical science teaches us that we must not dwell in sorrow. We must not lose hope. We must not gate our heart and our emotions and isolate ourselves from those who would love us. Guarding your heart is wisdom.

How to Mend a Broken Heart

Broken heart syndrome is real, and it can even be deadly. Yes, I said deadly. Medical science and cardiologists have found an amazing thing that King Solomon understood thousands of years ago: your heart health (and mine) is very much tied to how you feel emotionally. Broken heart syndrome, also called stress-induced cardiomyopathy or takotsubo cardiomyopathy, can strike even if you're healthy.[2] Women are more likely than men to experience the sudden, intense chest pain[3]—the reaction to a surge of stress hormones—that can be caused by an emotionally stressful event. It could be the death of a loved one or a divorce, breakup, or physical separation; betrayal; or romantic rejection. It could even happen after a good shock.[4]

In broken heart syndrome, a part of your heart temporarily enlarges and doesn't pump well, while the rest of your heart functions normally or with even more forceful contractions. Researchers are just starting to learn the causes and how to diagnose and treat it.

The bad news: broken heart syndrome can lead to severe short-term heart muscle failure.

The good news: broken heart syndrome is usually treatable. Most people who experience it make a full recovery within weeks, and they're at low risk for it happening again (although in rare cases it can be fatal).

The reason I am sharing this with you is because we need to understand that a woman's heart is a deep ocean of emotions, needs, and desires. The heart is the soul and spirit of a woman. It is her essence. And in matters of love, a strong woman with a strong, loyal heart can truly love back to life a good man whose heart has been badly broken. I know. I have witnessed it firsthand. It takes courage to love again when we have been hurt, but the best way to heal when we have been hurt is to dare to love again.

Let's face it, when we wound, we wound deeply. That's because when we love, we love completely. Guarding your heart is one of the most critical keys you can learn to unlock the secrets of your life. However, as human beings we often get badly confused about this Code. We think guarding is "gating," and it is not. Putting a gate on your heart after you have suffered a loss is a deception that will block your present opportunities and future possibilities at life and at love.

> Guarding your heart is one of the most critical keys you can learn to unlock the secrets of your life.

Author Henri Nouwen once wrote, "When those you love deeply reject you, leave you, or die, your heart will be broken. But that should not hold you back from loving deeply. The pain that comes from deep love makes your love ever more fruitful."[5]

Here is a brief true story to illustrate the point. When we think of 9/11, we rightly remember the tragedy and abject horror of the day. Yet I believe the single greatest lesson and takeaway from the events of September 11, 2001, is the redeeming and nurturing power of *love*. Love placed last-minute calls to loved ones saying, "I'll always be with you." Love fought back against the terrorists on Flight 93. Love ran into burning buildings to save women and babies. Love protected, rescued, and rebuilt a wounded nation.

On September 11, 2001, Andrew Bass was a thirty-two-year-old Brooklyn resident starting his second day at a new job downtown. He was a happily married man and the proud father of a thirteen-month-old son who was just learning to walk. His wife of eight years, Felicia, had so wanted a baby. After having suffered a miscarriage, at age thirty-six Felicia gave birth to their son the following year. Their lives were full. All was going according to their plans. Life was good for the Bass family.

That all changed when Felicia's office located in the World Trade Center North Tower was struck by a hijacked plane that morning, the first to be hit. She never came home. And Andrew was left with unfathomable grief, a young baby son, and the stinging heartbreak of losing his beloved wife to a national tragedy. Karen, a dear friend of Andrew's from college, was there to take Andrew's late night calls. Karen, who was single and a self-described workaholic, was always awake at night, so Andrew knew he could call her. Two years passed before Andrew wanted to live again. He invited Karen, his longtime friend and greatest supporter post-9/11, on a trip to Jamaica, and shortly thereafter they were engaged and married.

Fast-forward to now. Andrew's son, Sebastian, is fourteen, and his and Karen's daughter, Sofia, is seven. They are a family, and Karen is a mom to two amazing kids. And Felicia's memory is honored by them all as she lives on in her son. I think Andrew said it best in a 2011 interview I did with him for MSNBC's online magazine, "theGrio":

> "If we shut down and close ourselves off after a loss, in an ironic way we are diminishing the memory of those we loved," Andrew said. "Our loved ones would not want us to stop living. They would not want us to stay in a solitary moment in time. My life changed for the better because I opened my heart to love. I wanted to be fully alive again. From pain there is beauty after, if we allow ourselves to embrace it. You cannot walk around dead in a living body. Life is way too short. Live your life and in doing so honor the memory of the one you lost."[6]

Mending a broken heart is never easy, as Andrew said. There is no quick way to stop your heart from hurting so much. But to stop loving isn't an option either. Mending your heart means learning how to live with your feelings and move on despite them. Karen's story shows us that there can be love after loss. Birth after death.

Motherhood can manifest in many unexpected ways. Karen was forty when her daughter was born.

Here are five keys I took from Karen and Andrew's story, and ones that I myself have learned, particularly over the past year, on how we have to keep our hearts whole at all times. To deny our heart is broken is to bring emotional and spiritual death. Guarding one's heart means mending it when it's broken.

> Guarding one's heart means mending it when it's broken.

1. **Face it to fix it.** Denial leads to deep depression. Deal with the pain. Give yourself time to heal. Get professional help if needed.

2. **Spend time with you.** Reconnect with you. Rediscover yourself. Detach but don't isolate yourself from friends and family.

3. **Surround yourself with affirming thoughts, people, and circumstances.** Stay engaged in living. Your thoughts about you after a wounding are critical to how quickly you heal. Stay positive even when you don't feel like it.

4. **Help someone else who is hurting.** There is always someone who has it far worse than we do. Find people who are homeless, disabled, or sick with a terminal or debilitating illness and encourage them, read to them, lift them. It will lift you too!

5. **Learn from the loss.** Everyone we meet has something to teach us. When you are trying to heal, the best thing you can do is look for what you can learn from this heartbreak. How can you go forward?

These keys will help you to slowly get better day by day. I promise. I have been there myself. I had a devastating heartbreak in 2013 through early 2014. I am still working through it. But the key is to *work through it*. The thing to remember is that your heart health is vitally connected to your emotional wellness. You cannot separate the two. It is impossible. When your heart has been broken or you are grieving, you can take some steps to fight back and heal. By actively protecting and guarding your heart, and your soul, you replenish and continually renew your mind, body, and spirit connections.

Love People Who Will Love You Back

One of my favorite sayings is "know your front row" (see Code 17). Not only must you be diligent about guarding your heart, you must also surround yourself with people who will do the same for you. The people you love must love you back. The people you trust must be trustworthy. Love should be reciprocal, not one-sided. And although we can never know what someone will or will not do, if we choose our friends wisely, and make sure that they share our own Life Code, we are less likely to be hurt.

> If we allow the wrong people to wound us, we will miss the blessing of the right people who come to restore us.

All of us have been betrayed by someone we valued as a friend. This almost always happens because we refuse to see the glaring red flags. My grandmother used to tell me, "People cannot give you what they do not have." It took me some time to understand the truth of this wisdom.

Let me say it again: people cannot give you what they do not have. In a world of fast-moving people, gadgets, and unkind hearts, we must be careful whom we love and to whom we give our gifts. We must do so in a way that does not isolate us, wall us off, or make us afraid to be who we are. If we allow the wrong people to wound us, we will miss the blessing of the right people who come to restore us. Surround yourself with people who will protect your name, your reputation, your integrity, and most of all your heart.

Realize That Rejection Is Often Life's Protection

There is an old but powerful truth: people's rejection is God's divine protection. There are times when we must learn to celebrate someone's exit from our lives. The truth is that too many people are walking this earth "shattered." There is a big difference between being shattered and broken. You can recover from broken. But shattered is non-recoverable. My heart breaks for the people I have met who have allowed life to shatter them beyond repair. I have been close to that edge, as have many of us. But because I am surrounded by people who truly love me and are invested in my success as a human being, I emerge stronger after each heartbreak or disappointment. So, too, can you. Here are three keys you can use to help you better connect with people who will guard your heart:

1. **Get to know people.** We think we know people based on their Facebook profile, tweets, or otherwise. The truth is, we do not. The old-fashioned way of getting to know people still works best: Talk to them and get to know their family and friends. Find out where they work, if they go to church, if they engage in their community, and so on. Get to know people's Life Code. It will save you much heartache down the road. Take the time to get to know people for at least four seasons, or one year, before getting romantically involved or engaged in business partnerships.
2. **Know what you need.** One of the keys to relationship success is knowing yourself. What do you value? What do you look for in friendships and relationships? What is your love language? And what is theirs?
3. **Stick with the tried-and-true.** The people who have been in your life the longest and who are tested, tried, and true are the people you keep closest to you. Fair-weather friends, situational friends, and the like are not people you can trust. They will hurt you every time. Stick with what has proven successful over time. It will minimize damage, heartbreak, and brokenness.

Living the Code

Your heart is all about your Code. An open heart makes the world a place of possibilities. A closed heart shuts down all of those possibilities. If you hold on to hurts, pain, offenses, gossip, and pettiness, it will break you. Holding on to what has hurt us causes us to miss the blessings God sends abundantly before us. People who hold on to past hurts never quite get the big picture of their lives and of what truly matters. And they stay stuck. They never move forward because they are always focused on what someone did to them or what they have lost. It is a sad way to live.

As a result, they miss opportunities; they miss best friends; they miss financial blessings; they miss second chances at love. They are so busy guarding their hearts that they forget to give their hearts to those who are worthy of love. *(Don't miss that last sentence.)*

I read a great blog post last year by leadership training expert Michael Hyatt titled "Three Reasons Why You Must Guard Your Heart."[7] I recommend that you read it too because in it he captures perfectly three important things I have tried to emphasize in this Code: (1) the human heart is precious; (2) the heart is the source of all we do, for better or worse; and (3) the heart is continually under attack, so we have to be in protective mode daily from unnecessary barbs and hits.

A good leader strikes a balance between her heart and her mind. (We will discuss this at length in Code 14, Lead from Within.) If we lead with only our knowledge we will often miss the human element that is so important. As women we excel at empathy and compassion, classic "heart tools." Yet, if we constantly lead with our emotions and our heart, we will miss the important skill of protecting ourselves from harm and those who do not share our values or heart.

We all get hurt. It is a fact of life. But as my good friend Vicki likes to say, "Do you want to go through life with a boxed heart or a bruised one?" Her point is bruised hearts can heal. Boxed-off hearts are inaccessible. The goal is to live in balance. The goal is to love in healthy ways that don't lead to hurt. The goal is to identify the right people with the right values who know how to love us in healthy ways. The goal is to guard, not gate. The goal is to learn from our losses and use them to lead.

 ## Key Words

Heart	Guard	Forgiveness
Code	Honor	Vulnerability
Emotions	Empathy	Restoration
Feelings	Healing	Honor
Protection	Love	Resilience

Code 7

Be Resilient

Resilience is knowing that you are the only one who has the power
and the responsibility to pick yourself up.

—Mary Holloway

If we learned anything during the turbulent year that was 2020,
it was about the power of resilience. Resilience is everything.
Resilience is getting back up when you fall. Resilience is returning
to the arena of life when you have been knocked out of it. Every
woman possesses resilience, one of the Codes that is essential to
making it through the storms and disappointments of life. Resilience says to the world: You did not take me out. You did not dull
my shine. You did not snatch my hope. I still have better days ahead.
But here is the reality: if you live long enough life is going to test
you. If you don't master the art of being resilient, the challenges
of life will break you. One of the most important keys we must
have in the arsenal of living as women of our time is the power
of resilience. *Resilience* may be the most important word in the
human vocabulary after love. In some ways love and resilience are
closely linked, because when we love someone or something, we
will fight for them. We will stick with them. We will encourage
them. Stand by them. We will do anything to see them succeed in
life. Love, like resilience, means that we do not give up. And that
like the proverbial phoenix that rises from the ashes, we can dare
to rise each time we fall, no matter how hard we fall or how deeply
we may be hurt from that fall.

What I want to ask of you in this Code is to love yourself enough to fight for yourself. To get back up when you get knocked down. To find the courage to push through whatever it is you are going through. To never give up on yourself even when all looks lost. I want you to discover the hero in YOU. Because she is in there. She is inside of you. Sometimes we spend too much of our time looking for people around us and outside of us to help us through. There is nothing wrong with asking for help. But there are times when we must muster the willpower and the faith on our own to get back in the arena of life.

Love yourself enough to fight for yourself.

There will be times in your life when you feel alone. Your family may run, your friends may run, and your spouse and your kids may not understand. And all you will have is you and your faith. You and your Creator. You will have to find the courage to encourage yourself. You will have to talk to yourself. You will have to get up off of the floor, and you will have to crawl before you can stand again. I know because I have been there. And I suspect that before I am done living, I will be there once or twice again.

How do we learn to bravely and compassionately navigate the storms and seasons of our lives in such a way that allows us to develop an emotional set of boundaries, strengths, and attitudes that helps us to not just survive but thrive in spite of what life throws at us? In this Code we are going to talk about three keys that will help us develop resilience:

1. Discover resilience.
2. Understand how resilience works in your life.
3. Put resilience into practice in your life.

This Code determines how we bounce back when life throws us a curveball. So it is one that we must master and put into practice in our lives because we all need to be resilient in this journey called life.

Our innate desire to survive and to keep going no matter what happens is best exemplified in the holocaust of World War II. The Jewish people were being annihilated. They were treated as less than animals. They were tortured, murdered, and humiliated on a day-to-day basis for years. Families were torn apart. Fortunes were lost. Homes were ransacked. Children were starved to the point of death, then sent to the gas chambers. *The Diary of a Young Girl* with the writings of Anne Frank inspires generations of young female readers to this day, reading her words and feeling her spirit to keep living. Men like author Elie Wiesel (whom I had the pleasure to meet) emerged from the horror resilient. And they use their stories of survival to encourage the rest of us to keep living no matter what life hands us.

Discover Resilience

Resilience is the capacity to withstand life's stresses, challenges, and catastrophes. It is the ability to bounce back, to rise, and to cope when others fall apart under the same set of challenges. It is the ability to adapt. Resilience is like water. Water is persistent. It flows around rocks, valleys, stone, and mountains. It adapts to the conditions in order to keep moving. Some people have this ability and others do not. But I believe resilience is a set of skills and support networks that can be learned and developed when we understand how important being resilient is to our lives.

Resilience, then, is the ability to meet adversity in such a way that one comes through it unharmed or even better for the experience. By unharmed, I mean there is no permanent damage. But be clear, when we take a hit from life, we will suffer bruises, scrapes, and cuts that leave scars on our minds, bodies, and souls. The resilient woman, though, takes this in stride. She meets it with grace and not grief. I call it thriving.

I have a quote from the great Maya Angelou hanging in my office at home that reads: "Surviving is important, but thriving is elegant." I love this quote, because I, like millions of women the world over, have had to live it time and time again. The funny thing about life is that challenges don't come just once and then leave us alone. Challenges come at us daily, and some of life's greatest challenges (death, financial loss, illness, divorce, and so on) will come over and over again.

Resilience means facing life's difficulties with courage and patience—refusing to give up. It is the quality of character that allows a person or group of people to rebound from misfortune, hardships, and traumas. Resilience is rooted in the tenacity of your spirit—a determination to embrace all that makes life worth living even in the face of seemingly impossible odds. When we have a clear sense of identity and purpose, we are more resilient because we can hold fast to our vision of a better future. Much of our resilience comes from community—from the relationships that allow us to lean on each other for support when we need it.

> Resilience means facing life's difficulties with courage and patience—refusing to give up.

In March 2014, famed fashion designer, former supermodel, and longtime Mick Jagger girlfriend L'Wren Scott apparently committed suicide.[1] Here is a woman who seemingly had it all: great looks, a rich and famous boyfriend, a thriving business, a glamorous life. And yet, at forty-nine years of age she took her life. We may never know why, but the public speculation was that her business was not doing that well. The point is, where was L'Wren's support system? Her "front row" (see Code 17)? Did she ask for help? Was she depressed for many months and no one understood how deeply? Whatever the case, we know that a talented, beautiful, vibrant woman with everything going for her lost her ability to bounce back, to be resilient.

You see, resilience matters *a lot*. Resilience and happiness are closely linked. People who have close relationships and social support networks that can help them through times of adversity experience greater joy and satisfaction than those who do not. Such relationships keep us connected, covered, and protected during the bad times. Happiness involves so much more than feeling "positive emotions" versus negative ones. Happiness is made up of many different things. It comes and goes. Our happiness is rooted in our ability to bounce back again and again. I cannot say it any more plainly: *you can never be happy in life if you do not know how to successfully rebound from life's storms.*

Case in point, I know a wonderful young woman who lost her mom to breast cancer in the summer of 2012, lost her grandmother to the same disease six months later, and then was herself diagnosed with breast cancer that same year. The way she handled it still amazes and astounds us all. Most of us (me included) would still be on the floor. But not Kelly. She is pure faith, love, and resilience in motion. She beat the cancer, she beat depression, and she beat feeling sorry for herself (which she was entitled to) with an attitude of positivity that is unmatched. She spoke positive things over her life, she worked with her doctors, she had a prayer group, she called her pastor and church family for help, and she has a life row that was front and center in her journey. And she has emerged victorious and healthy. Now cancer free, Kelly is resilient.

Just as important is to find meaning and purpose when you reflect on your life. To live well does not mean that you will live a life free from adversity. Life is hard. We all deal with the same things regardless of our station in life, our ethnic origins, our religion, our politics, or our geographical location. We all suffer bouts of depression. We all bury loved ones. We all get brokenhearted. We all lose things. We all experience financial challenges. We all get sick. We all get lonely. Our loved ones get sick. Businesses fail. Kids disappoint us. Spouses leave us. It happens every day. Life can be hard, and hard times can break us if we allow them to do so. Make a commitment to develop a set of critical coping skills that will help to sustain you when the hard times come. Because trust me, hard times will come.

Understand How Resilience Works in Your Life

Resilience is not something you're either born with or not. Resilience is developed and eventually becomes second nature as we grow through the stages of our lives and gain better thinking and self-management skills and more wisdom. Resilience, in some ways, comes from how you were raised as a child, such as if you participated in sports, were raised to be a competitor, and encouraged to be brave. Our foundations in life (Codes 1–4) come from supportive relationships with parents, peers, and others, as well as cultural beliefs and traditions that help us get through life and cope (or not cope) with the inevitable bumps. Resilience is found in a variety of behaviors, thoughts, and actions that can be learned and developed as we grow older. Here are a few things about bouncing back and how we learn to do so that I have learned along the way and from some of the women I most admire:

Factors that contribute to resilience include:

- Having close connections with family and friends
- Knowing your value, your worth as a human being
- Being able to manage strong feelings and impulses
- Having good conflict resolution skills
- Being in control of your emotions and being accountable for your choices
- Daring to know when you need to seek help and support and to ask for it!
- Seeing yourself as a victor (rather than as a victim)
- Coping with stress in healthy ways and avoiding harmful coping strategies, such as substance abuse

- Having a vision and purpose for your life
- Finding the silver lining in life's bad news and bad events
- Having faith in your Creator

So resilience, then, is a learned behavior as much as it may be a trait with which we are born. My goal with this Code is to help you to build some resilience muscles that will give you the strength to get through some of the rougher patches in this thing called life.

Put Resilience into Practice in Your Life

Knowing what resilience is and where it comes from is nice, but what we need most of all is to put it into practice in our lives. In his bestselling book *The Resiliency Advantage*, the late Dr. Al Siebert, PhD, writes that "highly resilient people are flexible, adapt to new circumstances quickly, and thrive in constant change. Most importantly, they expect to bounce back and feel confident that they will. They have a knack for creating good luck out of circumstances that many others see as bad luck."[2] Siebert also notes that resilient people are good at seeing things from another person's point of view.

Here's the point: when we empathize with others, we feel less alone and less entrenched in our own pain. As a result, we recover faster. Connectivity with others, then (see Code 20), is a "key" tool to recovering when life hits us hard. More important to grasp, however, is that most psychologists agree that some people seem to be born with more resilience than others. But the good news is that they also believe it's possible for all of us to cultivate resilience if we are trained. One key is adjusting how we think about adversity (which goes to Code 11, Choose Your Thoughts and Words Wisely), how we process life, and what can happen in life, as well as being able to understand that life is not always going to be easy, but that when we come through the "process" we can emerge better, wiser, and stronger than before.

Resilient people are all around us. We see it in sports stars who get injured and have to start all over again to make it back into the game. We see it in singers, celebrities, and actors who hit a rough patch. They get on drugs, have a string of illicit affairs and ruined marriages, file for bankruptcy, and mess up their kids—and ultimately themselves—emotionally. Then they get the help they need and pull it all together once again. We root for these people. We want people to win. There is no greater story than that of someone who hits bottom and finds a way back up out of the pit, the muck, and the mire. How do they do it?

Resilient people have traits. They approach life and life's setbacks intentionally. They share very clear, distinguishable traits that we all marvel at as we see how well they bounce back from the worst that life can throw at them. In a *Huffington Post* article titled "How to Bounce Back from Failure—Over and Over Again," Carolyn Gregoire cites numerous sources and experts who study the power of resilience.[3] She outlines seven traits that resilient people possess:

1. They are realistic but are also optimistic.
2. They don't take rejection personally.
3. They create strong support systems.
4. They notice the "small," positive things of life, like flowers or running streams of water.
5. They practice gratitude daily.
6. They seek out opportunities to improve and grow as people.
7. They work through their emotions and feelings instead of avoiding them.

Living the Code

As we end this Code, I want you to assess yourself. Here is a great tool created by Dr. Siebert for determining how resilient you are and how you can work to develop better coping skills throughout your life.

Rate yourself from 1 to 5 (1 = strongly disagree, 2 somewhat disagree, 3 agree, 4 somewhat agree, 5 strongly agree). Then add up the numbers of each question and see your assessment below.

Q1: I'm usually optimistic. I see difficulties as temporary and expect to overcome them.

Q2: Feelings of anger, loss, and discouragement don't last long.

Q3: I can tolerate high levels of ambiguity and uncertainty about situations.

Q4: I adapt quickly to new developments. I'm curious. I ask questions.

Q5: I'm playful. I find the humor in rough situations, and can laugh at myself.

Q6: I learn valuable lessons from my experiences and from the experiences of others.

Q7: I'm good at solving problems. I'm good at making things work well.

Q8: I'm strong and durable. I hold up well during tough times.

Q9: I've converted misfortune into good luck and found benefits in bad experiences.

Less than 20: Low Resilience—You may have trouble handling pressure or setbacks, and may feel deeply hurt by any criticism. When things don't go well, you may feel helpless and without hope. Consider seeking some professional counsel or support in developing your resiliency skills. Connect with others who share your developmental goals.

20–30: Some Resilience—You have some valuable pro-resiliency skills, but also plenty of room for improvement. Strive to strengthen the characteristics you already have and to cultivate the characteristics you lack. You may also wish to seek some outside coaching or support.

31–35: Adequate Resilience—You are a self-motivated learner who recovers well from most challenges. Learning more about resilience, and consciously building your resiliency skills, will empower you to find more joy in life, even in the face of adversity.

36–45: Highly Resilient—You bounce back well from life's setbacks and can thrive even under pressure. You could be of service to others who are trying to cope better with adversity.[4]

🔑 Key Words

Resilience	Ask for help	Acceptance
Empathy	Get back up again	Love
Courage	Patience	Happiness
Faith	Outlook	Connected
Support systems	Perspective	Self-Awareness

Code
8

Age Gracefully

There is a fountain of youth: it is your mind, your talents, the creativity you bring to your life and the lives of people you love. When you learn to tap this source, you will truly have defeated age.

—Sophia Loren

My father was so captivated by Sophia Loren that he named me after her. Now well into her eighties, Sophia Loren is the epitome of agelessness, grace, beauty, wisdom, and poise. I love the quote above by her because it says it all: aging is a state of mind. Aging is what you think about. It's the talents that you possess, it's the creativity that you bring to the world. Ladies, it's time for us to stop being obsessed with youth. It's time to embrace the beauty, wisdom and fearlessness of aging.

To age is a gift. To age is to become wisdom and to wield the great light radiating from within you. To age is to be fearless. To mature. To grow more compassionate, more loving, and more complete.

To age gracefully is to share what you've learned from your failures and your successes.

To age gracefully means that you accept that aging is a part of living. You accept that your face may change. That your hair may grow thinner and grayer. That your body will wrinkle and that frown lines may appear. Yet, with each passing year, you learn to embrace each moment. You begin to appreciate the wonder and awe of life and the preciousness of what it means to be alive. You accept that the small aches will come and that you won't move as fast as you once did. It's okay, because if you are aging, my Sisters of the Code, you are living! If you're under thirty, please do not pass this chapter over or think it doesn't apply to you. Just keep living and I promise you with all of my heart that it will, someday it will.

One of the greatest things about being a woman is that, although we may operate by the same Life Code our grandmothers and mothers did when it comes to our core values, when it comes to aging gracefully I think we have learned a new way of embracing the life cycle as women.

To age gracefully means that you accept that aging is a part of living.

Everybody knows that 60 is the new 50, 50 is the new 40, and 40 is the new 30. We rage against age. We exercise, we stay fit, we run, jump, box, kick, fly, sail, lift, cycle, and climb. We say, "No, not me. I will not go gentle into that good night." But age we will, and age we must. How you decide to deal with the process will create either a rich and rewarding journey or a painful and lonely one. If there is one thing that women universally fear, it is the aging process. Youth is celebrated, elevated, and adored. Beauty is skinny, sleek, and tall. Smooth, fair skin or dark skin fitted with high, elegant cheekbones and chic, lush hair of varying lengths is what we worship. We are conditioned from the time we are tiny little girls to want to be beautiful. So when we are not, we are devastated. And we do all manner of things to become beautiful, and then to stay young and beautiful. And we often do so at the expense of our self-worth and value.

Here is the good news: we no longer have to fear aging. And it starts with an attitude, with acceptance. Yes, you will lose some things when you age. Life will change. I am living this right now in my midforties. But you will also gain so much more: perspective, joy, confidence, courage, self-love, assurance, a desire for peace, deeper connection with those you love, and freedom.

In this Code we are going to go through my strategies for the four areas of aging and learn how to embrace each area, encourage one another, and become better women at every turn. I want to help you to age gracefully, not just on the outside but on the inside where it matters. All of us have met someone who radiates light just beneath the surface of their eyes and their wrinkles, little old ladies who light up when they see other people or see their great-grandchildren. These women live long, I believe, because they free themselves early in life of needless distractions and life stressors. They run full throttle at life.

Author and motivational speaker Louise Hay has come up with an A to Z dictionary of certain ailments and diseases caused by our stressors in life. One of her best observations in her book *Heal Your Body A–Z: The Mental Causes for Physical Illness and How to Overcome Them* is the impact of physical and emotional pain on the aging process.[1] The research and science support the fact that negative emotions really *do* cause disease, illness, and premature aging. How can they not? The adrenal glands overproduce stress hormones, leading to suppressed immune function, illness, digestion problems, and poor liver and kidney function. They also cause pain and joint stiffness.

The two main keys for this Code, then, are:

1. Realizing that aging gracefully starts with acceptance
2. Living the Code: four strategies for aging gracefully

Realizing That Aging Gracefully Starts with Acceptance

Any discussion about aging begins with the word *acceptance*. The process of being born, living, and ultimately dying is a process of aging. The most significant thing any woman (young or old) can do to unlock the secrets of aging gracefully is to start with acceptance. You will age. Period. So take it in, make fun of it, and have fun with it. Aging is a gift. How many of us know women friends who lost mothers when they were young children or teens? How many of us have lost girlfriends in their thirties, forties, and fifties to breast cancer, heart disease, or other ailments? To be alive is a gift. Even when life may not be going so great, if you woke up this morning, you got a second chance at doing something you missed, or something on your bucket list, or a chance to say I love you or I'm sorry one more time. Each new day brings with it an opportunity to begin again. It's a fresh start every 24 hours.

The problem is that many women, when they get over forty, spend all of their time trying to look young, be hot, and be chic instead of being themselves. I spontaneously interviewed a couple of dozen men one evening at a large party in Washington, DC, and almost to a man they told me that there is nothing worse than a middle-aged or aging woman who is not comfortable in her own skin, who runs around in short-short dresses, super high heels, and clothing that tends to skew younger. In fact, many of these men at the top of their game professionally and in their thirties and early forties said they much prefer an attractive, confident, older, mysterious woman in every way, as opposed to being with a younger, beautiful twenty-year-old who doesn't know who she is or what she wants from life.

> Confidence, then, is an important virtue that will help us as we age.

Confidence, then, is an important virtue that will help us as we age. It's like a magnet to men at work, in the dating game, and in a marriage. Confident women are not to be confused with aggressive, overworked, stressed out *know-it-alls*. They tend to be turn-offs to men. But as we age as women, we tend to come into ourselves. Or as an old boyfriend's sister once told me, "Sophia, one day you will get comfortable with yourself and that will be a great day in your life." I did not understand what she meant then, but I most certainly do now. I enjoy my forties. In fact, as I said before, my power word for 2014 (I choose one every new year) is *acceptance*.

It's not a sexy word, or a deep word; it simply means we see life for what it is and what it no longer will be.

Acceptance is freedom. It allows us to move past our regrets, our mistakes, and our fears. Acceptance allows us to deal with what is, with what can still be, putting to rest what is lost. Age comes in seasons. We are children, then teens, and before we know it young adults. Our twenties blow by, then our thirties are ever so busy. Then our forties arrive and we begin looking back to see what we've missed instead of taking hold of what we still have ahead. Aging is not what it was in the 1800s, 1900s, or even the 1980s. Women look fit and well (without plastic surgery) into their sixties and beyond. As they say, 40 really *is* the new 30!

And menopause, which used to be viewed as the "death" of a woman's sexuality, sensuality, vitality, and value, is no longer viewed that way. Thanks to Gail Sheehy in her groundbreaking book *The Silent Passage* published in the 1990s, we no longer view it that way. Women date and marry younger men. Women have babies well into their forties now. Women are fit, fabulous, and fierce long beyond menopause. The fact is, most women face menopause, and Sheehy compellingly changed the paradigm about how society once negatively viewed a very natural, normal process for us as women and how we can learn to embrace it and shift to a new place in our lives as women.

One thing we need to accept more than anything is *each other*. I saw the most abject cruelty displayed during the 2014 Oscars regarding the physical appearance of former Hollywood A-List actress Kim Novak. Twitter was in an uproar on Oscar night when the eighty-one-year-old actress appeared to present with Best Actor Oscar winner Matthew McConaughey. Novak has clearly suffered some physical ailments (such as stroke), but her face has also been the victim of not-so-good plastic surgery, and the women journalists, celebrity photographers, and regular Janes were the most unkind of all.

It was relentless and disturbing, with Novak being called "plastic dummy," "wax mummy," "Scalpestein," and worse. Mostly at the hands of younger women, but some middle-agers chimed in too. What made the Novak flap so upsetting was how accepted it was for women to bash another woman for not being as pretty as she was at age twenty-five, thirty-five, or even forty-five. It was rude, crude, and downright mean. It is what made me want to make this Code one of the top 20 to unlock your life as a woman.

Living the Code

For this Code, I interviewed dozens of cross-generational women from all walks of life, ages nineteen to ninety-five. And I asked them if they had beauty secrets, daily facial/body regimens, special anti-aging ingredients, routines, certain foods, people they spent time with, family secrets, love secrets or life secrets, and more when it comes to how they embraced the notion of aging and doing so gracefully. Unlike other Codes, this section is more substantive as a wrap-up section to tell us how to successfully practice and live the Code.

Four Strategies for Aging Gracefully

Strategy 1—Physical: I am an Olay girl through and through. I have been faithful to their product line and have been using it since I was nineteen. Now that I am over forty-five, I use the Total-Effects 7 series of anti-aging products and Regenerist lines. And I have to admit being faithful to a daily cleansing, moisturizing, and toning routine has worked wonders. But let's be honest: your ethnic background, gene pool, and where you live all play a part in how well you age physically. Staying out of the sun as you age is key, as well as drinking lots of water, moisturizing, taking vitamins, calcium, engaging in weight-bearing exercises to build bone density after age thirty-five, keeping your BMI at a normal level, and leaving white sugar and flour almost entirely out of your life. These are the obvious things we all know to do, and more.

But what about your style from your twenties to your fifties? Here is some of what I heard: "Be age appropriate." "Have good taste." "You can still be sexy." What these women were saying is have fun, look fabulous, but determine what that means for your age. Look at some of the world's most admired women, from first lady Michelle Obama at age fifty-one to actress and former super-model Christie Brinkley at sixty, to Helen Mirren at age sixty-nine. These are all mature women, but they are in excellent shape, have healthy skin, and most of all have vibrant personalities. A good rule of thumb is, if you are not a teenager, don't dress like one. Men do not find this attractive; they find it pathetic. You also have to wear less makeup as you age, and keep it fresh, clean, and classic. Consider wearing short, chic hair versus long hair. Short hair accentuates the facial features. Long hair as we age tends to pull the face down. And watch those highlights. As we age, lighter (or gray) hair tends to wash us out.

The goal then is to take good care of your physical body, not necessarily to look younger but to look better. Be mindful of weight gain or loss that begins to creep up on you. Tend to aging spots. Quit smoking and sunbathing; neither is good for your skin. Honor your bone health. Get sleep, because it is critical to our wellness as women. Your looks depend a lot on your physical routine. Stay busy.

Various medical sources and research studies say that there are five important *sub-keys*, among many, to aging well:

- Being married; married people live longer and age better
- Having a healthy love and sex life
- Experiencing lots of laughter

- Drinking green tea, black tea, and, believe it or not, red wine. They are all super rich in antioxidants that doctors and scientists agree help with lessening the chances of getting cancer, heart disease, and Alzheimer's disease. And yes, of course ingesting dark chocolate absolutely lengthens the life span and helps with digestion and slowing the aging process.
- Taking care of your teeth and gums. Also consider whitening your teeth to renew your youthful smile.[2]

Strategy 2—Emotional: Acknowledging how you feel is important as you age. Whether we journal it, form book clubs where we can discuss it, or just share it with close friends, acknowledging where we are on life's journey gives us healthy perspective and possible solutions to dealing with aging. It's okay to have some feelings about the fact that you will not always be the young, pretty redhead in the room.

One sixty-seven-year-old I talked to, who is a beautiful Italian woman of five-foot-three and in great shape, said, "You feel betrayed by your body." But she countered, "Be grateful. Get perspective that you are lucky to be alive. You could be sick, disabled, or dead." Her point is that learning to manage your emotions around age matters. Your attitude determines a lot about how you will look in this life.

One forty-year-old quipped, "Complaining and whining are not good for you. They create negative energy." She speaks the truth, because as we know, "pain" of any kind, emotional or otherwise, is not healthy for your body, and worry ages the face and causes hair follicles to gray. Depression and inability to bond with and love others create illness and disease. In the end, you will age better if you face your life hurts and traumas. Deal with your sorrows. Don't run from grief or illness. Have faith and be intentional about your positive thoughts and words. The fact is, we can't run away from loss, and we can't run away from aging, so embrace them.

Strategy 3—Spiritual: I talked earlier about possessing a light that radiates from within your soul regardless of your age. It is your spirit that people either love or hate. A woman may not have a supermodel's looks, but I have seen many women land a handsome prince because she had that light that draws men. She radiates peace, calm, and compassion. She's not running around partying and drinking with her girlfriends. Conversely, I know many pretty women who cannot hide their petty hearts.

Your faith is another key component in how you age through the seasons of your life. Make time for exercise, meditation, prayer, naps, short breaks, relaxation music, walks at lunchtime, connection with nature, and spiritual things. Tap into your creativity. Having a good life balance allows you to tap into your right brain—the calmer, more peaceful, and artistic you. Practice keeping mess and clutter out of your life; it blocks your positive energy. Alleviate drama. Be introspective. Keep perspective. Surround yourself with people who bring you peace and joy. Focus on being present versus always looking behind you or ahead of you.

Strategy 4—Relational: Last, in my opinion, the ultimate key to aging well is to have good lifelong friendships and connections that serve as your support network. There are well-documented, proven health benefits of being close to our family, friends, and colleagues, and of attending social events. There are over fifty million single adult women in the United States alone and billions worldwide. Yet we need connection like the air we breathe.

Do not be alone for long periods of time. Get out and do things. It is also important to have continuity and consistency in our relationships, meaning we keep people around us who know our history and who can be trusted. Most important—and I practice this—be open to younger friendships and connections. Look for the new, good, and interesting things of life. Embrace that love can come again even in your later years.

I met a woman and a man who found love at sixty-four for her and seventy-one for him. They have a ball together. They are married. They enjoy travel, exercise, and have a robust love life.

There is still a lot of life ahead of you even when you are in your seventies and eighties.

The great secret to aging gracefully, then, is this: you don't change. Your body does, but you are the same in many ways, so stay young inside. Embrace change. Say good things; practice compassion; have peaceful, loyal, loving people in your life who bring those virtues to your private space. Do not live in the past. We all need something to look up to, to look forward to, and to chase.[3]

The final word on aging is this: You cannot obsess over what you can no longer do. You have to focus on what you still can do.

Key Words

Age	Spirit	Joy
Beauty	Emotions	Creativity
Grace	Faith	Thoughts
Elegance	Love	Pain
Acceptance	Health	Grief
Acknowledgment	Laughter	Dis-ease (leads to
Calm	Peace	disease)

Section III

The Spiritual Codes

Every woman has a spirit. The spirit part of us is often the part we neglect most. Spirit is not religion. Spirit is not a bunch of rules. Spirit is what keeps you on track to nourish your soul and be a light to all who come across your path. These four Codes are simple, but they are powerful when put into practice in your daily life.

Code 9

Do Not Gossip

Whoever gossips to you, will gossip about you.

—Spanish proverb

Gossip is truly one of the most evil, ugly, damaging things that any of us can participate in or be party to hearing. If I was only allowed to give out one piece of wisdom before I take leave of this earth, avoiding gossip and gossips is the advice I would give most passionately. I have seen gossip destroy relationships within my own family. I have had career doors shut on me because of the lies of a gossip. I have been shunned and whispered about by people who have never even met me. No doubt, you have experienced this, too. We all likely have been lied about, lied to, or manipulated by the ugly scourge of rumors and gossip.

If it is so commonplace, is it really that bad? In a word, absolutely! Gossip is a cancer of the human soul. It ravages the mind, the spirit, and if taken to its awful end, even the body. Gossip is a poison, and we have found no antidote with which to eradicate its devastating effects. We have all been the victim of someone's gossip or slander. And sadly, we have all gleefully carried a tale or two of someone else's demise. Gossip is a cancer of the human soul.

Some years ago, I was the subject of the most relentless and ugly gossip campaign. It began with a simple misunderstanding over the cost of shipping some books left over from a women's conference. I did the event as a last-minute request from a friend,

I didn't take an honorarium, and one of my corporate partners paid for my flight. I was happy to do it.

Long story short, our staffs got into a tiff over who was responsible for paying for and shipping the leftover books. Texts started flying and legalese was thrown about. To keep the peace, I paid for the shipping, apologized for any misunderstanding, and moved on. I thought the matter was over, but it was not. I received an inflammatory text from my friend, and I called her to talk. She refused. Emails started flying. Name-calling ensued in emails between my publicist and my friend. It was awful. Trying to be a woman of honor, I apologized again, I took the financial hit, and I even tried to get some mediators involved to try to repair the breach between us. It was not to be. What happened next is what I want all of you to heed as we talk about the soul-searing damage of gossip.

What started in private went public. She held briefings on me, telling other women not to speak to me or deal with me. Some women stopped speaking to me. Some unfriended me. Some listened and also began to attack my reputation. In frustration to try to clear my name, I tweeted, held sister chats, and even penned a three-part online magazine series for Essence.com entitled "Sisters, It's Time to Heal," trying to address the issue and the pain I felt.[1] The series struck such a nerve that I did national radio and TV interviews. The series was nominated for a journalist award in 2013.

But the catalyst for how this small thing turned into a big thing happened at the hands of a woman who knew us both. She played both ends against the middle (that is what gossips usually do), stoking a smoldering flame into a raging fire. How silly we both must have looked to her. How powerful she must have felt. Making two women, supposedly dedicated to helping to elevate and teach other women, fight, scratch, and tear down each other.

Let's pause and reflect: Two women who were once good friends had a private disagreement. It was settled quickly. But because of tempers, ego, poor communication, no conversation (see Code 19), immature staffs, and foolish pride, it turned into a major incident that was escalated by a gossiping interloper. *Do not miss what I just shared*, ladies. This is the danger of gossip and tearing down other people. The sting of gossip lasts forever. And the damage, once done, can never be undone.

Gossip is like a seed. Once planted, it puts down strong roots. What began as one woman's personal smear campaign exploded. People who did not know me "heard" all about me in social, church, and professional circles everywhere. I tried to get the truth of what really happened out; I even went back to the same city a year after the first incident happened for a second women's event, but it was futile. In certain circles, the damage was done. My reputation was sullied and in tatters. And worst of all, a lot of potential very positive relationships, lifelong friendships, and professional connections were forever lost.

Here's the lesson: You cannot chase down gossip. You cannot repair a ruined reputation once gossip has had its way. I had to learn that the hard way. Once someone has formed a certain "opinion" of you or heard slanderous talk about you, *nothing* you do will be right. Every move you make will be scrutinized, and you will be suspect. You simply cannot win against rumors. Your best bet is to just keep living an honorable life and let your character defeat the lies. The truth will eventually come to light by your positive living.

> Gossip is like a seed. Once planted, it puts down strong roots.

I share this personal and still painful story to illustrate a crucial point: *Gossip is deadly. It is destructive. It is uncontainable.* That is why we must be so careful with our thoughts and our words (see Code 11). Gossip emanates from a deep place of envy, pettiness, and unchecked anger. It comes from a soul that is bitter and broken. It comes from a coward who is unable to confront someone so she takes to the "airways" of gossip.

It is wrong to try to destroy a woman because you "do not like her" or because you did not have a "good experience" with her. And it is up to the rest of us to call out this kind of mean-girl behavior when we see it. In my situation, I watched good women sit passively by and not call this woman out because they feared her title and position. That is what gossip does: it makes onlookers passive partakers in the destruction of another woman's name.

> It is wrong to try to destroy a woman because you "do not like her" or because you did not have a "good experience" with her.

In this Code we are going to look at three important keys that will help you to get a better handle on gossip and effectively keep it away from your life as much as you can:

1. Gossip defined
2. Why we love gossip
3. The collateral damage of gossip

Gossip Defined

So what is "gossip" anyway? Let's break this down upfront.

1. Gossip. Noun. Casual or unconstrained conversation or reports about other people, typically involving details that are not confirmed as being true. Rumor or talk of a personal, sensational, or intimate nature.[2]
2. A person who habitually spreads intimate or private rumors or facts.
3. Trivial, chatty talk or writing.

Gossip has been around for millennia. Gossip, in my opinion, is one of life's greatest temptations. In the book of Exodus, God warns us away from gossip. The notion of bearing "false witness" against another person is *so bad* that it made it into the Ten Commandments. In Proverbs 6:16–19, the Bible records that there are six things the Lord hates and that the seventh thing is detestable to him. What is that seventh thing? Gossip. A person who divides others. A person who causes havoc between others by her words. The Hebrew word translated "gossip" is defined as "one who reveals secrets, one who goes about as a talebearer or scandalmonger." A gossiper has privileged information (or makes up information) about people and proceeds to reveal that information to those who have no business knowing it. Gossip is distinguished from sharing information in two ways:

1. **Intent.** Gossipers often have the goal of building themselves up by making others look bad and exalting themselves as some kind of repositories of knowledge.
2. **The type of information shared.** Gossipers speak of the faults and failings of others or reveal potentially embarrassing or shameful details regarding the lives of others without their knowledge or approval. Even if they mean no harm, it is still gossip.[3]

I witnessed one of the best illustrations of these definitions I ever saw when I was a teenager. The minister at our Vacation Bible School brought out this very large fan, a pillow, a wood board, and some tar. He took the tar and spread it on the wood board. Then he cut the pillow open with a knife (very symbolic) and turned on the fan. The feathers began to blow everywhere, but most of them stuck to this tar-covered, wooden board. After about two minutes, the minister turned off the fan and told us in a very firm yet quiet voice, "This is what gossip looks like in action." We immediately understood his point: *gossip once spread is unstoppable.* And worst of all, *it sticks.* Like a feather blown about by a strong wind, once it finds a sticky surface, it is impossible to remove that feather. Cutting the pillow with a knife symbolizes what happens. When you gossip about another woman (human being), you are in fact gutting her like you would a fish that has been caught and is being prepared to be cooked and eaten for dinner.

I know we think some gossip is just harmless banter and innocent giggles. *But it is not.* When we only have half-truths and partial facts, we end up with the wrong story. And it does untold damage that often cannot be repaired. So the next time you laugh about another woman's weight and her obsession with food, STOP. When someone comes to you to "innocently" share some seemingly harmless gossip, *stop* and ask yourself these five hard questions:

1. Is this TRUE? Did I ask the other woman her side of the story?
2. Would I say this about my mom, my sister, or my best friend?
3. Do I actually know this person? Does this sound like her character? Or is this out of character?
4. Would I like someone to blackball, malign, slander, or gossip about me in this way? No is usually the answer.
5. Is this about the fact that we (or I) don't like this woman? (If you don't like a woman, just let her be. If it is in the professional context and she worked for you, then speak lawfully and truthfully only about her performance, not about her character or her personal life. Don't seek revenge for whatever wrong you suffered at her hands.)

Gossip comes from people who are entrusted with secrets and choose to violate that trust. It comes from busybodies who run around with "information" (sometimes true and sometimes false) and take joy in adding to that information. But really gossip comes from a much deeper, "spiritual" place. Gossip, as the Scriptures point out, has been in our hearts from the very beginning. And it is a work of evil.

I know that may sound harsh or overly religious. But stick with me for a minute. One of the Greek names for Satan (aka "the devil") is "slanderer"[4] or "false accuser." Think about that. The most notorious "being" ever known to humankind has at the root of his name the meaning of a gossip: one who spreads slander, accusations, or false things. When you gossip, you are making an accusation. You are spreading information, whether true or false, without the permission or the knowledge of the subject of your gossip. Slander is a higher form of gossip. It raises defamation of one's character to a legal level. Slander is so bad that it can be redressed in a court of law. To slander is to knowingly and falsely spread something about someone. However, to tear down someone to others, to berate them, and to attack them is, I believe, ultimately to ruin yourself. Sooner or later, if you continue to be the bearer of tales, accusation, and false information, people will want nothing to do with you for fear they will be your next victim.

Why We Love Gossip

Whatever the root causes of gossip, one thing is for certain, we love a good piece of "scoop." We love to hear "stuff" about people. It all seems harmless and innocent. But psychologists say it is both very damaging and very common.[5] And the root of gossip, according to psychologists, is that "gossip builds social bonds because shared dislikes create stronger bonds than shared positives."[6] Our DNA is apparently wired to be drawn more to disliking someone than bonding over shared positives. Psychologist Laurent Bègue says that two people who don't know each other will feel closer if they share something mean about a third person than if they say nice things about them. But let's delve further into the psychology of why we as women seem to love to gossip much more than men.

Author Rosemary Black wrote an amazing piece titled "10 Reasons Why Women Love to Gossip," which gives us great insight into why we gossip. Here is an excerpt of what she wrote:

> Whether it's a whispered conversation over coffee with a friend or a late-night telephone gabfest with your sister, gossiping bestows a feel-good aura on women who are feeling stressed-out, jilted or just

having a bad day. And while it's been criticized as idle chatter, or worse, gossip is beloved by women everywhere. If you're wondering just what women get out of dishing on others, and why it feels so completely satisfying, here are the top 10 reasons why women just can't stop themselves from indulging in one of life's naughty little pleasures:

1. Gossip gives women a feeling of fitting in with others.
2. Gossiping helps you make friends.
3. Gossip reduces stress.
4. Gossip helps us process our experiences.
5. Gossip helps validate our feelings.
6. Gossip helps you deal with everyday life.
7. Gossip is a great way to network.
8. Gossiping is a learned trait that we observe in others.
9. Gossip lets women dissect relationships with other women.
10. Gossip makes us feel a little guilty.[7]

The Collateral Damage of Gossip

In its simplest form, collateral damage means that we do damage to things or people that are incidental to our intended target. Collateral damage is what happens when we gossip. Mutual friends and acquaintances are tainted. And people are drawn into a mess that has nothing to do with them. Our human nature is to side with our friends, even if we know they are in the wrong. We fear that if we don't join in with the abuse being heaped on another woman, we may become the next victim of such talk. Sisters of the Code, this is not who we are. We have to think before unleashing our wrath on another woman who has offended us or simply made a human mistake. This goes to Code 19: we must learn to have conversations with people before we condemn them or cut them off.

I lived through this. It has hurt me deeply to see women I once admired, women with whom I wanted to work, and women I supported and helped, or who once had a good opinion of me succumb to the cruelty of character assassination before they ever had a chance to get to know me. Gossip is all about destruction. And it claims many victims. To gossip about another human being is to be intentionally unkind and cruel. But to gossip about another woman is *breaking the Code*. It is breaking the timeless Sister Code that unites us. People who gossip, listen to gossip, or both are lazy. They don't believe in fact-checking. They don't believe in the power of positive confrontation. They don't believe in the protection of people's reputation. They just like to spread information.

A mature woman understands that to indulge in gossip, no matter how seemingly insignificant or innocent, is to indulge in destroying reputations, connections, friendships, and professional alliances. I have seen careers ruined and personal lives destroyed by gossip from other women. We are often our own worst enemies. And it has to change.

Let me close by saying that I, too, like to laugh. I like to cut up. So I am not suggesting you can't tease with your friends about your colleague's wild new hairdo. What I am suggesting is that there is a very FINE line between poking fun and gossiping. It plays to our most base instincts and desires to be part of the crowd. Women of the Code don't care about the crowd. We care about the Code. The best rule of thumb to follow as much as it depends upon you is to just let gossip pass you by.

Living the Code

Here are my **10 reasons** you should never gossip and tear down another woman behind her back, and **3 actions** you can take to STOP gossip at the start (and challenge and correct the bearer of such gossip).

10 Reasons You Should Never Gossip

Reason 1: If you engage in gossip, chatter, or slanderous statements about another woman, I promise you it will get back to her. The people snickering with you will share that you initiated such talk.

Reason 2: You don't want to be gossiped about. So don't do it to others. Period.

Reason 3: If you feel you must "warn" someone about a person with whom you had firsthand experience, then proceed with the disclaimer that this was YOUR experience; it is based on fact, not rumor; and that you are warning that person because you want them to be careful about how they engage with this person in the future. Then let them decide.

Reason 4: Just because someone else hates her does not mean you should. You will block your possible blessings if you allow gossip to keep you from getting to know a woman you do not know but about whom you "heard" something.

Reason 5: When you tear down another woman, you look bad. People don't trust you.

Reason 6: It's unkind and "unsisterly" to attempt to ruin another woman's reputation because you don't like her or because you fell out with her. Let people learn for themselves. Go back to Reason 3. If it applies, that is different.

Reason 7: In the workplace, gossip about people's salaries, personal lives, or private conduct is off-limits. If the HR staff finds out, you could find yourself unemployed.

Reason 8: If you are a Christian or person of faith, it is against your Code to gossip. Godly people do not engage in slander or gossip. Period.

Reason 9: People watch what you say and do as a leader. If you don't walk what you talk, people will call you on it.

Reason 10: People can change. Give them a chance. Show grace and mercy to people just as YOU (and I) need it. Women of the Code are abundant in grace.

3 Actions You Can Take to Stop Gossip at the Start

Action 1: Confront a gossip with the wrongness of her deeds. A gossip must be confronted in order to be constrained. If you entertain a gossip you become no better than her. Maybe she does not understand. Maybe she has never been corrected. Don't be afraid to help people do better. Confront gossip with respect, but confront it head-on at the beginning.

Action 2: Shut it down. Say, *This is not what I do. It is not who I am. I will not listen to or entertain this type of discussion behind someone's back.*

Action 3: Lead by example. If you are in a leadership position, it is critical that you lead by example. If you hear about gossip, blacklisting, and so on, you must address it in the open and shut it down. And as a leader you can never be engaged in bad talk about others. It completely destroys your credibility.

The key to dealing with gossip and gossipers rests in finding the courage to confront people. Gossip is a social disease. The only way you eradicate disease is to cut it out. Gossip must be immediately cut out. Then and only then will we be able to trust one another as a sisterhood and support one another up the ladder of success—not just in business, but in this journey we call life.

Key Words

Gossip	Hearing	Destruction
Tearing apart	Seeing	Interlopers
Dividing	Believing	Conversation
Fact-Checking	Uncover	Confrontation

Code 10

Apologize Quickly

A meaningful apology is one that communicates three R's: regret, responsibility, and remedy.

—Beverley Engel, author, *The Power of Apology*

We live in an age unlike that of our mothers, grandmothers, and great-grandmothers. We don't apologize. They did. We don't understand the power of saying "I was wrong." They did. We have bought into social media bravado and Facebook rants. They had no such distraction from the graces and codes of civil life. We are much more transactional. And it has taken a huge toll on our families, our friendships, and our souls. But let me tell you what I know for sure—apologies matter. A lot. They help us. They heal us. They give us hope that we can do and be better and free ourselves from unnecessary drama. Sisters, life is dramatic, but it is rarely like a Hollywood script.

"Love is never having to say you're sorry." What a great line from an even greater movie, *Love Story*. The problem with that line is that it isn't true. It's a romantic notion of what love should be versus the reality of what love is. Love and apology are intricately linked. To love is to be willing not only to say, "I'm sorry," but to say, "I am sorry and I am ready to make right whatever I have done wrong." Love is to say, "I am ready to change."

The ability to apologize is a key virtue that, if learned early in life and practiced faithfully, will bless your life and lengthen your days. It will build your family. It will nourish your children. It will comfort your spouse. It will create safe havens for your relationships. It will protect and honor your friendships. And it will heal, defuse conflicts, and cover people in ways untold. The ability to apologize, and to do so quickly when we are wrong or have caused offense, is a balm more powerful than any medicine. An apology is an affirmation that says, *I value you. I heard you. I wronged you. I care about you. And I want to be restored to you.*

I cannot stress enough, Sisters of the Code, how important it is to apologize, sometimes even when we did not do the wrong. Sometimes we apologize to restore peace and to fight for our relationships. Always choose your relationships over a need to be right. You can find yourself right and all alone. Never forget that. It is the truth. In our modern culture we are obsessed with the notion of "forgiveness," but we rarely want to talk about how we get there. To most of us forgiveness is looking at what someone did to us and what they owe us: an apology. But rare is the person who looks in the mirror and says, "I messed up. I was wrong. I need to make this right." Rarer still is the wise woman who understands that there is power in offering an apology when she is the offender.

All roads to redemption start with an apology. The person who perpetrates the offense usually operates in two schools of thought: (1) that she did nothing wrong, or (2) if she did, she does not care. The offender never walks around bruised, broken, and hurt. It is the person who suffers the wrong, the perceived slight, or the offense who gets stuck in the pit of anger, sadness, and unforgiveness. What I want us to learn is how we can play a part in protecting the people we love and work with—from *us*. That's right, you heard me. We need to protect people from our words, our actions, and our wrath.

> All roads to redemption start with an apology.

One of the greatest books I ever read was a gift some eight years ago from a sorority sister who had offended me deeply. We were close friends. Our moms were close friends. But she had a serious problem with gossip and a lack of discretion. The thing I liked about this sister, however, is that she was very good at accepting correction. She was, as my friend Michigan-based counselor Dr. Sabrina Jackson likes to say, "coachable." After we had not spoken for about six months, I got an unexpected package in the mail. It was the book *The Five Languages of Apology* by Dr. Gary Chapman. Inscribed in the book was this:

Dear Sophia, thank you for loving me enough to tell me when I am wrong. Know that I love you enough to admit it, and say that I am sorry. I pray you will forgive me, I was jealous of you. I had to admit that to myself. That is my issue not yours. You are the best friend a woman could ever have. Please read this book and know that I plan to honor our friendship going forward.

Of course, I was touched by the gesture and the inscription. And I let her know it. First, I acknowledged her apology. Then I accepted her apology. And finally I wrote her back and told her I would read the book and pray about restoring our relationship at some point. Although I ultimately decided not to restore the relationship as it once was, for a myriad of reasons—less having to do with her and more to do with where I was in my life at the time—I appreciated her efforts and I learned something powerful. I learned that it takes great humility and courage to admit when we have done wrong. It takes even greater courage to ask someone to restore us, forgive us, and take us back. To offer a sincere, contrite, and well-thought-out apology is to give life back to someone we have hurt. Yes, I said, "to give life back," because when we intentionally or unintentionally injure someone we take away a little bit of life.

Let me explain. We are all human. We are all fragile. As we discussed in Code 6, Guard Your Heart, we have to protect the source of our life, the wellspring of our life, and that is our heart. Our emotions. Our soul space. Our relationships. The reality, however, is that if you and I are going to deal with other human beings, we are going to get disappointed, hurt, mistreated, and sometimes worse.

But we can learn the tools to help us to better navigate relationships. One of those tools is the ability to apologize and to do so quickly. The premise of *The Five Languages of Apology* is this: apologies are central to maintaining and healing our relationships. Learning how to apologize can be of tremendous benefit. Some books on anger and forgiveness focus on what to do when the other person offends you. Chapman's book talks about what you need to do when you offend others and when you need to ask for forgiveness.

In this Code we are going to look at three powerful keys to help you thrive in this important spiritual area:

1. What an apology is
2. Why apologizing matters
3. How to offer an apology and regain trust after an offense

These three keys are essential to your success as a leader, as a spouse, as a friend, as an employer, as a coach, as a sibling, as a parent, and most importantly as a human being. If you can find the wisdom to learn these keys and use them regularly when conflict arises, you will soar and thrive in all areas of life. **Bottom line:** it is one thing to accept an apology; it is another thing to offer one.

What an Apology Is

In its most basic form, an apology is saying "I am sorry." The problem is, we often stop there and we do not own our mistake. We do not try to learn and grow from it so that we won't cause injury or hurt those we care about again. Saying "I'm sorry" is easy, but an apology is so much deeper than that. An apology takes ownership. An apology offers respect. An apology says, "I didn't honor who you are and who we are as friends." An apology says, "Your feelings matter to me, and I don't like that I have hurt or injured you." An apology says, "I want to make this right, if I can. I want to change my behavior and restore our fellowship."

An apology is not saying, "Sorry you are angry." Or "Sorry you took it that way." Those are dismissive words that add insult to injury. Those words pierce the soul and they cause even greater offense. If you cannot offer an effective and honest apology, it is better to keep your mouth shut. An apology does not lay blame, dodge responsibility, or avoid the person you have hurt. An apology is a powerful force that can bring about great healing, purpose, knowledge, and personal growth. The challenge for most people is that they don't know the basic elements of an apology. In my opinion, an apology requires these ten elements:

1. Humility
2. Compassion
3. Respect
4. Connection
5. Contrition
6. A heart seeking peace
7. Ownership of your actions
8. Passion
9. The willingness to change
10. A purpose or end result

These ten elements are common sense, and they are universal. They help us to learn what we need to communicate when we need to mend a rift, restore a relationship, or rebuild a bridge. To offer anything less to the person whom we have offended is to come off as inauthentic, self-serving, and careless. An apology has power because it instantly shifts the energy from a place of pain to a place of possibilities.

Why Apologizing Matters

Now that we know what an apology looks like, let's talk about why it matters so much that we apologize when we are wrong and that we do so quickly. To me this is very simple: an apology matters because it allows the injured party to heal. In Code 9 I talked about the offense of gossip that was committed against me. Ironically, the offender attempted to approach me a year after it happened through a mutually trusted mediator to talk. I was open to the conversation and agreed to take part. In fact, I felt an instant rush of relief when I knew we were going to speak. I was still very hurt. She knew that what she did was wrong (she confessed it to others), but because of her ego, position, and pride, she let it go too far. We never had the conversation; she was advised by someone in her camp not to speak to me because she would be possibly admitting legal liability. To be honest, that was the furthest thing from my mind. I wanted closure. I needed to audibly hear her say, "I am sorry that I hurt you, and I am willing to make amends for the damage I did to your good name."

The apology I sought never came. There was no healing. In fact, I think the hurt deepened for me.

My point is this: I spent a lot of precious time being offended and angry by what had happened. I kept trying to make right what I had not made wrong. It made me bitter, untrusting, and at times mean. And because I was still connected to people who were connected to her and who celebrated her "image" versus what we all knew had happened, it only deepened my wound. Sometimes you have to make a clean break from people who are still connected to painful events from your past until such time as you can heal and truly release the pain.

I stayed pretty angry for almost two years. I was literally made sick by the stress I was carrying. As a woman of faith I was spiritually hurt by this event in a very profound way. But the truth of the matter is this: I needed to know why. I needed closure. I wanted answers. I wanted to know why a trusted friend, whom I loved like my sister, would hurt me so. It is an offense that I am still trying to make peace with and truly release years later. I promise you that had we talked that day, had she tried to contact me, had we cried, yelled, listened, forgiven, and at least parted ways peacefully, I would have been okay. I just needed to hear her say, "I am sorry."

So you see, an apology really matters. It matters to the person we have hurt.

In reality, though, most of us will never get an apology we are owed. And if we don't find a way to work through it and make peace with it (see Code 2), then we can get stuck. We need apology like we need air. Our spirit knows when it has been violated. And it seeks justice. It wants to be tended to and comforted. The point is, we are hardwired for apology because there are actual physical and emotional benefits to both offering an apology and receiving one. An apology is essential to our mental and even physical health. Research shows that receiving an apology has a noticeable, positive, physical effect on the body. An apology actually affects the bodily functions of the person receiving it as well as the one giving it—blood pressure decreases, heart rate slows, and breathing becomes steadier. An apology also has enormous emotional benefits, like the release of anger, fear, shame, the inability to sleep, and regret.[1]

How to Offer an Apology and Regain Trust after an Offense

An apology has to have a goal in mind. And that goal should not be to assuage your ego or to get rid of guilt. The goal of an apology is to offer acknowledgment of an offense and bring healing to another's wounded soul. Most people do not know how to offer a proper apology. I only learned the importance of getting this right after reading Dr. Chapman's book. There really is a formula, according to Chapman, on how we offer an apology. There are five elements of apology:

1. Expressing regret—You must say: "I am sorry."
2. Accepting responsibility—You must admit: "I was wrong."
3. Making restitution—You should ask: "What can I do to make it right?"

4. Genuinely repenting—You should commit: "I'll try not to do that again."

5. Requesting forgiveness—You must ask to be restored: "Will you please forgive me?"[2]

More important than the mechanics of how to offer an effective apology is making sure that what we say connects with the offended and that what happens psychologically and emotionally for the person is restorative and healing. Here is a list of seven necessary outcomes (though there are more):

1. The person's dignity and humanity are *restored*.

2. She feels *affirmed* by your admission that a wrong was committed.

3. She is *validated* by the fact that a wrong was acknowledged.

4. You offer a promise of *change* that protects the aggrieved party from further injury.

5. There is *justice* for the wrong act committed or public restoration if she has suffered public embarrassment or humiliation.

6. The victim receives some form of *compensation or consolation* for her pain.

7. A *conversation or process* takes place that allows the offended parties to express their feelings toward the offenders and even grieve over their losses.

Let me add this caveat to the above list: there are times when no matter how sorry we are and how much we want to make things right, we cannot. And apology, frankly, in some cases may not be enough. Sometimes the wound is just too deep. But here is the thing to remember: your only responsibility as a fellow human being and as a person of spirit is to be accountable for your actions (see Code 5), to apologize, and to offer to make things right if you can. If the person you have offended does not or cannot accept your apology, you are free. You are clear. Learn the lessons and let it go.

Living the Code

I will end where I started: love has everything to do with saying you are sorry. Love, friendship, relationship, fellowship, mentorship, and sponsorship require that we own our actions, both the good and the not so good. Offering an apology can be hard; it gets down to putting aside your ego and your pride. It is worth repeating: *always choose your relationships over a need to be right.*

We do great damage to our families, our kids, and our colleagues at work by not possessing the character and Code to apologize quickly when we are wrong. Why do I say apologize quickly? Because when you get into the core of who we are, *pride* is our biggest weakness. If I can quickly own something that I have done wrong, I can recover from that wrong even quicker. If I allow denial, pride, or guilt to set in, I will delay doing what I know is right. At the expense of another person's rights and dignity, I will protect my ego versus admitting my fault or transgression. By owning our words, our deeds, and our shortcomings, we are proving that we are growing. We are proving to ourselves and those who are in relationships with us that we get it. That we are adults. That we want to live by a Code of honor, integrity, and humanity.

None of us should want to travel through this life alone. None of us should take pride in the fact that we can callously hurt or discard people and leave them on the ground wounded. What we as a sisterhood of women need now more than ever is empathy and compassion. We need to own our actions. We need to be accountable. We need to put ourselves in another woman's shoes. Apologize when we are wrong. And dare to grow to a better place of understanding, compassion, and sisterhood.

🔑 Key Words

Love	Compassion	Humanity
Apology	Empathy	Validation
Humility	Ownership	Reparation
Integrity	Sisterhood	Acknowledgment
Honor	Accountability	

Code
11

Choose Your Thoughts
and Words Wisely

By words we learn thoughts, and by thoughts we learn life.
—Jean Baptiste Girard

Once you say it, you can never take it back. Sadly, we are living in the age of "cancel culture"—the age of "mean" and "mean girls" on social media. We are in a challenging space as human beings now that we have the power to immediately dispense our thoughts and our words behind the deceptive anonymity of a keyboard or phone. Our words and our thoughts are linked together. Whatever I am thinking, if it sits long enough, will come out of my mouth. And these thoughts will then become my deeds. And if we do not choose carefully what we dwell on, and what we ultimately choose to say, we will forever find ourselves in turmoil. In relationship distress. In business conflict. How we think and how we speak defines who we become.

The Bible says, "Words have power in matters of life and death."[1]

But before a word is ever uttered, it begins as a thought. So it might be fair to say that the power of life and death resides in our thoughts.

The power of what we think about is immense. Your thoughts and mine determine much of our life's successes, failures, choices, and actions. But the mind can be a tricky thing. It can be a battlefield of positive and negative feelings, past memories, and future desires. That is why it is so important that you "think" before you speak. Choosing your thoughts intentionally and then measuring them carefully before they become your words is critical, not just to your own well-being but to the well-being of others around you.

That is what this Code is all about: connecting your thoughts and your words. If you operate by this very important Code, your days will be long, your relationships will stay blessed, your business will thrive, your career will flourish, your kids will honor you, and your spirit will be at peace.

> Everything we are, everything we say, and everything we do starts in our hearts, in that most private soul space.

To ignore this Code, however, is to spit out your words in haste, in anger, and with a poison more deadly than cyanide. Sadly, we have all done it. Your words can become someone else's inspiration or heartbreak. Your thoughts come from whatever is residing in your heart untapped, unspoken, or unresolved. That is why in Code 6 we looked at the importance of guarding your heart, because everything we are, everything we say, and everything we do starts in our hearts, in that most private soul space.

In this Code we will look at how your thoughts become your words and how your words ultimately become reality—and not just your words but those words that were spoken over you as a child or as a young adult, as we covered in Codes 1 and 2. What we think, we begin to speak and ultimately act out. Here are three keys we should all consider:

1. How we form thoughts
2. How words shape our reality
3. How to be intentional about our thoughts and words

Every woman has been on the receiving end of mean words that have wounded her deeply. Some of the words spoken over us as children or as young adults carry their sting well into our adulthood and old age. Likewise, we have all been on the receiving end of great words, encouraging words, and life-giving words. Those words have great positive power in our lives. A word of correction can help us shift onto a positive path. A word of love or apology can soothe a broken heart or restore a lost friendship. A word of inspiration can help us walk through the valleys of life. And a word of gratitude lets us know that the good we do here on earth is not in vain.

When we understand how our thoughts and words connect, we can use both to propel ourselves and those we meet to greatness. If we can learn to harness the power of our thoughts and words, nothing in life—and I mean nothing—is out of our reach.

How We Form Thoughts

Do you control your thoughts or do they control you?

If you, like me, believe that you at your core are spirit, then you believe your thoughts are a manifestation of your heart, your emotions, your experiences, and your faith system. If, however, you prefer a more scientific approach, then you believe that thoughts are formed as a result of how the brain interprets emotions, which are themselves purely physical signals of the body reacting to external stimuli. Dr. Antonio Damasio's groundbreaking research in neuroscience has shown that emotions play a central role in social awareness and decision making. His work has had a major influence on our current understanding of the neurosystems that underlie memory, language, and consciousness.[2]

An example: I had a serious bicycle accident in the summer of 2013. I sustained blunt trauma to my abdomen, had a swollen spleen, and was in the hospital pretty banged up. The physical pain I felt was a direct result of the accident. *That makes sense.* However, the emotions I felt about what happened manifested in several ways. I cried, I suffered frustration at the loss of my mobility, I felt sadness and fear that I needed help up my stairs and even into my bed for a few weeks. Each of these emotions began in my private thoughts and then were expressed in my communication to others.

What I felt emotionally had a direct link to my physical experience. Yet, it doesn't end there. To form a thought has to be more than physical. The Psalms are rife with passages about "thoughts" and "feelings" that have nothing to do with physical pain, but instead with the pain of betrayal, loss, adversity, and love. It seems logical to me, then, that deep in our DNA, in our human Code, we are hardwired for both. We are wired both to feel and to process those feelings. Then those feelings become our thoughts, then our words, and finally our actions.

We've all experienced heartbreak, whether an unwanted breakup of a relationship or the death of a loved one. But did you know that being "heartbroken" is more than just an emotional response or feeling? Being heartbroken has real physical manifestations and symptoms.[3] Being heartbroken can literally kill you, as I outlined in Code 6.[4] Your brain reacts to heartbreak the same way it does to physical pain. That is why we say it hurts when we suffer a loss; *it literally does hurt*, even though we have sustained no physical injury.

Ironically, one of the reasons it can hurt so badly is that we keep rehashing our memories. We play old songs, we look at photos, we reminisce about the love we once had. And this floods our bodies with stress hormones that can cause a sudden heart attack, pneumonia, gastrointestinal problems, and more. The power of choosing what we dwell on in our thoughts is enormous. Our minds are receptacles for memories, experiences, emotions, feelings, hurts, joy, love, and pain, all of which form our thoughts.

Author Elizabeth Gilbert writes in her *New York Times* bestselling *Eat, Pray, Love*, "You need to learn how to select your thoughts just the same way you select your clothes every day. This is a power you can cultivate. If you want to control things in your life so bad, work on the mind. That's the only thing you should be trying to control."[5]

I agree, but before we can control our thought life, we need to understand how and where our thoughts come from. You cannot control what you do not understand. My goal is to help you to understand your thoughts and how you get them, so that you can take control of them and use them to your greatest advantage.

How Words Shape Our Reality

The power of life and death is in our words.[6] That is an *aha* statement if ever there was one. When we speak, we give power. What we speak, we send forth. It's like an explosion of sorts. Our words form into energy. If you wake up each day and tell yourself that you are ugly, have no worth, will never find love or achieve your goals—guess what! You are right.

Our words tell the world who we are, what we think, and how we feel. Once a thought has formed in our minds, good or not good, it is going to come true. As one of my mentors used to tell me, you will only truly get to know a person when you see them operate in the midst of pain, struggle, adversity, loss, or even great triumph. His point was that when people get squeezed by life, what comes out is what has been sitting inside. So be careful of your words.

Two Women: Words Made the Difference in Their Thoughts

Stephanie is twenty-seven years old. The eldest of three kids, she grew up on a farm. She is a junior executive (yes, at twenty-seven). Stephanie's mom died when Stephanie was fifteen years old. Before she died, her mom told Stephanie, "Stay positive. Your thoughts create your life. What you say to yourself and to others will define your life." She practiced her mom's advice intentionally throughout college, and as she began her career as a whiz kid at age twenty-one, she told me she wanted to "honor my mom's memory by being a woman of grace and positivity."

She made a decision to choose her thoughts and her words carefully. She was intentional about who she wanted to be, how she wanted to feel, and more importantly, what she wanted others to get from her.

Stephanie recruits for her company. I asked her new husband why he married her. He answered with a big smile, "That is so easy. She is the most positive, affirming person I know." Stephanie's story could have turned out differently if she had not chosen to control her thoughts and her words. She could have gotten mired in depression, pain, and sadness at the sudden loss of her mother. She did not. She chose life.

Phyllis, age sixty-five, is retired. She is single, has no children, and lives with her two older sisters, who are twins. Phyllis and her sisters grew up in a negative home environment with low expectations for the children. Both of her parents were decent people; life had just been hard on them. Both her mom and dad spoke negative words to each other, they cursed, they argued, and they did the same to and in front of their daughters.

Phyllis and her sisters went to a small school where expectations were low for girls. Phyllis was good at math and science at a time when girls were not encouraged to be. Ms. Davis, her ninth grade teacher, encouraged her to attend college and get a good job with the federal government. Phyllis told me that Ms. Davis probably saved her life. When her parents died, she and her sisters had no money, no inheritance; they just had each other.

The positive and affirming words Ms. Davis spoke to Phyllis helped to push her past the pain and get to her purpose. Phyllis became an award-winning researcher who helped our government make amazing strides in women's health and wellness. She credits the shift in her life to a schoolteacher who saw something great and believed in her.

Phyllis and Stephanie are extraordinary human beings. They both had women in their lives who spoke words of impact to them.

The words of these older women propelled them to accomplish great things. The power of life and death is truly in our words, and our words become our actions. Moms, please take heed of these examples of the power you have to impact your children with your words. What we say around the young people in our lives *matters*. Our words last forever. Words are more powerful than a punch. They can push others to greatness or wound them forever. So be careful. Be intentional with your thoughts and spoken words.

How to Be Intentional about Our Thoughts and Words

To be intentional is to be deliberate, resolute, and firm, to fix your mind on something and to follow through. When we learn to harness the power of our thoughts and words, we are unstoppable.

The power of intentional thinking happens when you *actively decide* how to think about a topic or situation. If, at seventeen, I decide to think about becoming a doctor, and I talk about being a doctor, I read medical books in the summers, I go to college and take pre-med courses, I intern in hospitals, I work in a doctor's office, I apply to medical school, I get into medical school, and so on, I will eventually become a doctor. The power of my intention starts with what I choose to focus on and speak into existence in my life.

Most successful people would agree that their success is due in large part to their ability to be intentional about what they want, how they pursue it, how they value it, and what they are willing to sacrifice to obtain it, whatever "it" (the desired goal) is. You can take control of your thoughts, your emotions, and your words by tweaking a few things that you do daily.

Your mind is the most powerful tool on earth. It brings to life the issues of your heart. Your mind can be a creative force for brilliance, innovation, and transformation. Or your mind can be a dark place that holds on to life's unfairness, losses, and wounds. Whatever your mind thinks, one thing is for certain: your words will follow. As the Scripture says, "The mouth speaks what the heart is full of."[7] Your thoughts and your words are first cousins. They are inextricably linked one to another. You cannot have one without the other. Your power rests in your ability to focus your thoughts and to train them in the way you want them to go.

Living the Code

Every choice we make has a collateral effect on the people we love, work with, and interact with daily. One of the hardest tasks on our journey is to look deep within to see who we are—not how the world sees us but how we perceive ourselves.

Our thoughts matter, so we need to be conscious of how we are thinking about ourselves and others. I learned the following two exercises in my own sessions with a professional coach back in 2004. I have modified and adapted them to better help you to understand how you perceive yourself and how you process your thoughts into your words. If you want to change your life trajectory, you must change your thoughts.

Exercise 1: Make a column titled "How I see myself." Write down the first words that come to mind. Next, consider what you have written. Then look at the list below and underline those words that best fit how you see yourself.

Do you consider yourself:

Beautiful	Ugly
Smart	Stupid
Sacred	Plain

Superior	Inferior
Competent	Incompetent
Outgoing	Introverted
Brave	Cowardly
Open	Closed
Emotional	Isolated
Compassionate	Selfish
Understanding	Impatient

Think about the characteristics you chose. Now go back and look at each word, and after each word say to yourself, "I see myself as _____, and this is a choice I have made because . . ." By looking at how we perceive ourselves we can then move on to examine the experiences occurring around us and see if we can link the two. If we create our experiences by how we think, then we are also able to change our experiences by altering our thoughts. We have no limits except the ones we place on ourselves.

Now review the words on your list and decide if you want to continue looking at yourself that way. If not, then circle that word. This time, you will speak each word out loud, and as you do, say to yourself, "I can choose to continue seeing myself as _____, or I can choose to focus on my natural gifts and positive virtues instead."

The point of this exercise is to get you to focus on how you think and feel about yourself. Everything about us emanates from how we value or do not value ourselves. Go back to Code 1 (Know Your Value) if you are having problems controlling negative thoughts and words in your life.

Exercise 2: Write down what you think about in the early morning and before you go to bed. Those thoughts set the tone for your day and for the next day.

Every day for twenty-one days (it takes that long to form a habit), I want you to journal one or two pages on what you think about in the morning and at night. You will learn so much about the state of your life, your mind, and your words.

Here is a sample of my routine.

- I linger in bed. I understand that if you have small children or a spouse who is talking to you, or something needs your attention, this can be challenging. But try to steal a few moments in the morning to be still. It centers you. It wakes you up peacefully.

- I pray before I do anything. Some of you meditate; that is fine. Just get still and focused. Get quiet. Let your mind wake up to empowering, lifting, encouraging thoughts.

- I don't let distractions enter my space early in the day. Keep TV, radio, and noise to a minimum. This keeps your thoughts focused versus reacting to the physical stimulus of bad news, arguments, and so on. Maya Angelou called it "guarding your sacred space."

- I journal. I have accountability prayer partners, and I practice Code 6 (Guard Your Heart) in ways that I never have before. I guard my heart, my soul, my sacred personal space.

These exercises will help you to control your thoughts. If you are allowing your thoughts to control you, your life will be a nightmare. Your words follow the thoughts, emotions, and feelings of your heart. Understanding this connectivity and how powerful your thoughts are is life changing.

Key Words

Thoughts	Active	Emotions
Words	Reactive	Feelings
Mind	Peace	Heartbroken
Body	Accountable	Change
Impact	Guard	

Code
12

Never Cut What
You Can Untie

Never cut what can be untied.
—Portuguese proverb

My paternal grandmother used to say, "Baby, never cut what you can untie." And I would say, "Nana, what does that mean?" She would smile and tell me that one day, when I was all grown up, I would understand. Fast forward to my swearing-in ceremony for the Bar of New Jersey as a new, young attorney. At the reception, Nana took me aside and said, "Now that you are a grown woman, the best advice that I can give you is to never cut what you can untie." She explained, "It means simply to not burn bridges in your life unnecessarily so. It means that there is a time to cut and a time to simply untie." Her wise and timeless advice has always stayed with me.

Life rarely presents us with clear-cut situations. In our relationships, things become even murkier because relationships are all about negotiation. How do we get what we want and give someone else what they want? How do we ask for what we need and communicate what we feel? Relationships require much negotiation and navigation. If we don't master the art of courageous conversation, being accountable, and being authentic—combined with knowing our front row and guarding our hearts—we will fail at building lasting and meaningful relationships.

We make decisions daily about whom we like and whom we love. It's called weighing your options, knowing what you should and should not value. Like the old Kenny Rogers song, life is all about knowing when to hold your cards, play your cards, or fold them and walk away. There is a time for cutting and there is a time for untying. The smart woman knows the difference. And she lives by its wisdom.

When we operate by a Code, life comes into focus. A Code gives us nonnegotiable principles that form the center of our lives. There are times when we must extricate ourselves from certain people. We "untie" in order to step back. We take a deep breath. We exhale. When we untie, we're saying to ourselves and to that other person, you still matter to me but right now I need to let you go. Untying gives us the option of tying it all back together in the future.

If, however, we make the decision to remove ourselves from certain people or situations, we are making a commitment not to go back but to move forward. Untying says I want to still be connected to you, but I need some space right now.

Cutting severs a bond. Cutting should only be done after we have exhausted all other options (unless, of course, we are in any type of immediate emotional or physical danger), particularly when we're dealing with people we love. We get caught up in our emotions and fail to communicate what we really mean. Instead of communicating, we react, often wrongly and hastily, leaving hurt feelings that can't be mended. I have "cut" very few things in my life. If I "cut" off something or someone, it is only after great thought, great prayer, even greater effort to talk, and a very clear indication that my Code is being violated.

In this chapter, we will dive into the art of relationship negotiation when your heart is involved or when your career may be on the line. *Cutting vs. untying is a skill.* Successful, savvy, sophisticated women use it all the time in navigating treacherous workplace and professional networks. And even when it comes to our families, which give us our most sacred and intimate relationships, knowing when to walk away or cut unhealthy ties is crucial. Code 19 (Have Courageous Conversations) will help you to learn how to make these types of healthy decisions when it comes to facing the inevitable crossroads of relationship management and when to walk away from people forever or just for a season.

Something that has helped me is to embrace the truth that people don't stay the same. We choose different paths that sometimes require us to release someone we once valued. My grandmother used to tell me when I was a girl, "Baby, never cut what you can untie." I had no clue what she meant until I became a woman. What she was saying was this: once you close a door, burn a bridge, build a wall, speak a mean word, or break a heart, that relationship is likely lost forever. My goal in this chapter is to help you keep the right doors open, to walk across the bridge again if you need to, or to cut something and truly leave it behind. We are going to use three simple keys:

1. The value of untying
2. The power of releasing and cutting
3. Determining when to cut versus when to untie

The Value of Untying

People make mistakes. Because we are human and fallible, we have to think long and hard about what it means to give people second chances. The old saying goes, "People are in our lives for a reason, a season, or a lifetime." The value of untying is simple; it means that we still have hope for the good we see in the relationship. We all want second chances in life when we make mistakes. We all need grace and forgiveness in abundance. And we also must be willing to extend that grace.

Imagine this: Take a piece of thread, tie it to your wrist, and then to the wrist of another person. Leave about a foot between you. Pull it tight. Your arms are linked together by this thread. When you're ready you can simply untie the thread and go your separate ways. No harm done. The connection has not been permanently severed. You still have a whole piece of thread that allows you to connect again if you desire. Now instead of untying the thread that holds you together, cut it in two. You no longer have a single strand that binds you and you no longer have a piece of thread that can be mended because it has been cut. If you use a sharp edge, the cut will be clean, two pieces, separated forever. But if the scissors are dull the separation will be "messy." The ends will fray.

My point is this: Untying allows us to reconnect. Untying gives us options. Untying allows us to reconnect later if we so choose. How do you know when it's time to untie someone or something from your life? I use three rules that I learned from my professional mentors and from my internal Code.

Rule 1: Consider the pros and cons of this person in your life. Ask yourself, What is the value of this relationship? This requires that you know what you want, what you need, and where you are going. This assessment can only happen when we think clearly. This rule must be followed when deciding whether to leave or sever a relationship, particularly if it is a long-term relationship.

Rule 2: Read all the cues, think through the possible outcomes, and then decide whether it is worth your while to continue. Ask yourself, What are the possible repercussions or collateral damages if I disconnect from or untie from this person or situation? One of my mentors taught me to ask the questions no one else dares to ask and to see what is unseen in any given situation. In Code 9 (Do Not Gossip) I broke this down pretty clearly. There is always "collateral damage" when we exit relationships the wrong way. It will have ripple effects that could cause unintended damage for a very long time.

Rule 3: If you love this person and value the relationship, then save it for another day. Ask yourself, Can this relationship be salvaged, mended, or restored? If whatever has to be untied for now has a hope and a future, then let it be. If you are a person of faith, give God time to work it out. Have a courageous conversation and ask for some time apart to heal, to reflect, and to grow from whatever has hurt you.

Untying is wisdom in action. It is making a decision to *err on the side of caution*. It is understanding that some things must be handled with grace and not with grief. How you exit a relationship is as important as how you begin a relationship. How you release people matters. A famous Maya Angelou quote sums it up well: "People will forget what you said, people will forget what you did, but people will never forget how you made them feel."[1] Untying is conflict resolution coupled with the art of negotiation. Try it before you cut.

The Power of Releasing and Cutting

Some actions speak so loudly that no words are needed. Some relationships cannot be mended because they are like glass; when broken, the pieces can harm you. Believe people when they show you who they are, and act accordingly. If someone shows you love, kindness, and generosity, then believe that is part of her Code. If someone shows you she lacks integrity, honor, and loyalty, you should likewise believe that is part of her Code. The difference between cutting and untying is all about Code. Remember that your Code is who you are; it is the compass of your life. It must never be violated for any reason.

There will come a time in your life when you will need to "cut" whatever it is or whoever it is that is toxic in your life. There will be no looking back. NO second chances. No crossing of bridges. It will be finished. It will be done!

Before I get into the meat of this section, let me give you three rules for knowing when it is time to cut for good:

> **Rule 1: If this person or situation violates your core Code, cut them or it immediately.** If someone I love, befriend, or trust intentionally lies to me or intentionally deceives me, we are done! There can be no negotiating with a bad Code. Lying goes to character. Deception goes to character. Do not try to negotiate with or fix someone's bad character. It's not your job to do so.

> **Rule 2: If you are in immediate physical, emotional, spiritual, or financial danger, cut!** Let me break this one down. Women stay in physically abusive relationships out of fear. People stay in bad jobs out of fear. Courage must challenge fear. Remember your value. Be brave. Love yourself enough to teach people how to treat you (see Code 3).

> **Rule 3: Don't cut in anger or when hurt.** What will be the collateral damage of cutting? The greatest temptation about cutting is to do it in anger or when we have been deeply hurt. Cutting is like surgery. It should be done with precision, skill, and as a tool that cauterizes the wound to minimize bleeding. *Remember this*: forgiveness is greater than vengeance, and compassion is more powerful than anger.

> Forgiveness is greater than vengeance, and compassion is more powerful than anger.

Determining When to Cut versus When to Untie

Two Professional Women: One Cut; One Untied

Lisa is a thirty-seven-year-old entrepreneur who employs five people. She specializes in helping companies grow through mergers and acquisitions. Lisa is single, and she cares for her elderly father, who is her only relative. Lisa's strongest quality is her ability to connect with people and build powerful networks. She has a big heart and lifts other women regularly.

Lisa contracted to do business with a major New York law firm that specializes in mergers and acquisitions, where her friend Joan is a partner. Lisa's accounts receivable are set up to be paid 50 percent at the start of a contract and 50 percent at the end. The firm, through Joan, agreed to the terms verbally and in writing.

Lisa got a big job off-site that required travel. Despite the fact that she did not get the required 50 percent deposit to start the work, she did the job out of respect for Joan, who got her the opportunity. Lisa got rave reviews on her work and returned home very pleased because she was asked to come back again. But weeks turned into months and she was still not paid by the firm. After two months, Lisa was informed by her HR person that the matter needed quick resolution or the company would suffer a shortfall. Lisa immediately went to Joan and asked her to intervene. Joan agreed. Unknown to Lisa, however, Joan was having problems in her division with cash flow.

Weeks went by and Lisa received a scathing text, followed by a menacing call, from Joan. Lisa was both stunned and deeply offended. She had known Joan for over a decade. Lisa's business had been severely impacted by the delay, and it caused problems with timely payment for her father's home-care services. She called in a trusted mutual colleague to try to mediate the fallout and reached out to some trusted mentors for counsel. It was obvious Joan was under some pressures that had nothing to do with Lisa. She had already started to try to blackball Lisa, and word got back to her. Ultimately, Joan apologized and pledged to make things right. Lisa accepted her apology but is now afraid to do more work with Joan. What should she do? Cut or untie?

Here is the lesson: Lisa's first instinct when she received Joan's call was to respond in kind. But upon further reflection and after receiving wise counsel, she realized that she could not cut off her relationship with Joan completely. Cutting would have negatively impacted her business and other professional alliances the two women shared. So what Lisa did was untie—step back and renegotiate her relationship with Joan as a friend and as a client. Lisa also reinforced her internal contracts process and set up better business processes to prevent a repeat scenario. She untied versus cutting in anger. Lisa was not treated fairly by Joan and no longer trusted her. But by stepping back, untying, and renegotiating her relationship with the firm, she got more work from the client and made even greater contacts, which led to many more positive opportunities for her. In this case, Lisa's decision to untie was the right choice for both her and her business.

Alexandra is forty-two and is a conference planner. She is energetic, hardworking, and always looking to help and support other women. Alex was approached by a friend to do an event with a third party she did not know. The event had a quick time line, a modest budget, and demanded many hours. She hired two young women for this special project who begged for the opportunity to work for her.

The things Alex was promised by these two women were not delivered, deadlines were constantly missed, and poor communication methods were the norm. Alex had to clean up their mess and deal with the fallout from the other major partners. She fired them both. Unbeknownst to Alex, one of the partners decided to hire one of these ladies and use her on a project where Alex was involved. She did not tell Alex about it and hid the fact that this woman was paid with funds Alex had raised from sponsors.

Alex found out from a mutual colleague, who had been told about the "secret" alliance in confidence and who was very upset by the subterfuge. She was right. Alex needed to know that someone she thought was a partner deceived her. Alex secured all of the sponsor dollars for the event, and the person she had previously fired was getting paid with these funds by the partner. Alex was beyond angry. They used her contacts, her brand, and her media access to have a successful event, but they misappropriated a sponsor's money.

After the event, Alex requested mediation with all parties. Her goal was to recoup the sponsor's money. The partner dodged her. Alex then sent a certified letter to the partner and her board, documenting the ethical breach and professional breach. She severed the relationship with this partner immediately! What Alex did not do was gossip. She cut it. She put it behind her and learned a hard lesson.

Cutting was absolutely the right choice in this instance. Bad character, lying, and deceiving others is never something we can negotiate or fix. Once someone's Code has been corrupted it infects everyone and everything around it.

These two real-life stories prove the point of this Code: your Code governs your conduct and how you handle your associations and relationships with others. Lisa encountered what we call a "hiccup" with Joan. Joan is not a bad person who is malicious or deceptive. Joan did not know how to properly communicate her internal administrative challenges to Lisa. Joan erupted and took out her failings on Lisa. Humans do that sometimes. We get it wrong. Lisa and Joan will mend their wounds and they will move forward wiser. We must extend grace as we need it.

Alex took some hits, but she gained something far more valuable. She learned that someone she thought was a friend, sorority sister, and partner had very bad character. After making sure that she stated her feelings about the betrayal, she released it and never looked back.

Both women teach us what to do and what not to do to minimize collateral damage. This Code is huge in our lives. It relates directly to Code 1: Know Your Value. How we value ourselves relates to Code 3 (Teach People How to Treat You).

The Code of your life, like your DNA, is uniquely connected and interconnected. When faced with conflict or a decision to cut or untie, ask yourself these three questions:

1. Is this a project or a relationship? Meaning, is this a badly broken person I will keep having to try to fix, excuse, or manage?
2. What part did I play in this? People only do what we allow them to do.
3. What is the condition of their heart? Look at their fruit. What is their Code?

Living the Code

How we exit a relationship of any kind matters. It matters how we talk it out, untie it, or cut it. You will save yourself a lot of trouble if you live by a Code and deal with people who share your Code. According to Nicole Roberts Jones—an author, a national motivation speaker with Motivating the Masses, and a leading coach for professional and entrepreneurial women—here are three key things we need to keep in mind when we are faced with making the decision to cut or untie.

1. **What are the deposits and withdrawals of this relationship?** How does this relationship add value to your life or make you feel?
2. **Believe people when they show you who they are.** If you see the condition of a person's heart and it is rife with malice, ill will, and unkindness, you need to believe it. If you see them treating someone else poorly, it is only a matter of time before "them" becomes "you."
3. **How you release people is critical.** You are releasing for you and not for them. So do what you need to do to clear your soul

space. Don't be abrupt. Withdraw slowly. Preserve people's egos if you can. It minimizes the damage they can do with other people in your networks, or socially.[2]

Anytime you have to devalue yourself to accommodate the relationship it is time to release or cut it. This gets back to Code 1 (Know Your Value). You must not allow anyone to devalue you. When people hurt you beyond your capacity to heal, you must cut them. Cutting isn't always bad. We all agree that untying is preferable. But sometimes you must cut things off. Women are taught to mend, restore, and forgive. Men are taught to obliterate and cut. That makes women more likely to tolerate unacceptable behavior, which destroys our self-worth. You cannot cherry-pick character. Your Code is not up for negotiating.

People's hearts are exemplified in their behavior. It is so crucial, then, for us to recognize and make good decisions about how to release toxic behavior. Don't spend your precious time holding on to people you should cut. And don't let a moment's anger cause you to cut what can be untied.

Key Words

Negotiate	Value	Untying
Cut	Code	Bridges
Tie	Thread	Heart
Self-Worth	Connection	Choice

The Professional Codes

Successful women are intentional. They live by powerful Codes that integrate their personal, spiritual, and professional values into a winning strategy for all. They lead at work as they do at home—with heart, compassion, sisterhood, smarts, and savvy. That is what makes women unique.

Don't Think Like a Man

We need to understand there is no one formula for how women should lead our lives. That is why we must respect the choices that each woman makes for herself and her family. Every woman deserves the chance to realize her God-given potential.

—Hillary Clinton, from her address to the United
Nations Fourth World Conference on Women

Since I wrote the original Woman Code book, a woman was the nominee for president of the United States, and now one is vice president of the United States. Both of these trailblazing women are intelligent, bold, savvy, and powerful. They didn't listen to the naysayers. Or to those who told them to wait their turn. The secret to their success—and yours— as women running in the circles of men: own your power. Be you. And understand that the first rule of being a woman is to understand that you are *not* a man.

Now it may seem kind of silly to you that I would say this, but it isn't. We have long lived in a world, particularly as it relates to us as professional women, that demands we act like one of the "boys" in order to move up, move ahead, and be accepted in the workplace. Such nonsense has now crept into our dating and romantic lives, with bestselling books and movies with titles like "*Act Like a Lady, Think Like a Man.*" Ironically, however, when we do behave like men in the workplace, we are dubbed the "B" word, or worse. We are "too aggressive," "too hard," "too ruthless," and "not a team player." And if we "play the game" like the men do when it comes to dating, we are labeled "loose" or "on the prowl." We can't win.

We all know the career girl stereotype.

But what we don't talk about is what this kind of stereotype can do to the sisterhood of women. We all know the career woman who stays to herself, doesn't really like other women, definitely doesn't mentor or support other women, and sits in her corner office suite, hair in a bun or blunt bobbed, glasses on, middle-aged, not very nice, and hard.

She's that woman in *The Devil Wears Prada*.

She can curse like one of the boys, drink like one of the boys, and she definitely acts like one of the boys. She never gets emotionally attached. Yet, the problem is, no one likes her very much. She doesn't even like herself. This woman was sold a bill of goods long ago that she had to act like a man, dress like one (she only has three colors in her closet: black, gray, and navy), and be one in order to succeed. It was part of her generational upbringing. She conformed to what she was told to do if she wanted to be a "career woman."

The problem is in trying to think like and act like a man, such a woman has lost the true transformative essence of her power. And her power comes from the mysterious, sacred, and creative space of being a woman. This type of woman has been tricked into believing that women are powerless and that we have nothing good to offer of our own merit. She believes women cannot have it all: love, marriage, kids, friends, and career. Or that a woman cannot choose not to get married and have kids and still be a woman just the same. That is false, and a belief that we as a universal sisterhood of women must constantly work to replace with the truth of where our power comes from. Power can never be given, or even transferred. True power comes from within.

Stasi Eldredge, coauthor of the book *Captivating: Unveiling the Mystery of a Woman's Soul*, explains that all of us women are still little girls somewhere within, holding on to our dreams of love, romance, beauty, and adventure. We are warrior princesses wanting to be both independent and whisked away by our prince on his white horse.[1]

If what Eldredge opines is true, then we are defined most of all by our relationship to men, to our dreams of being swept away, and in being pursued because we are beautiful. *I disagree strongly* that this is all a woman desires. I do, however, believe it is part of what we desire. Stop and think about this for a minute: if our core identity as women is tied up in our relationships and in how we look, whereas men's identity is wrapped up in achievement, success, and competition, then is it any wonder we struggle with guilt and self-condemnation when we pursue something else outside of those proscribed relational boundaries?

Sure, men want love and romance too. But it is not the first thing they are taught to value or identify with. This presents a challenge for women when we want to step outside the proverbial box and take on leadership roles, create a business, or focus on things outside of the home and our relationships with family and friends. So we have to redefine what we want and what we teach our daughters to want from life.

Just imagine if a woman wrote a book titled *Act Like a Man, Think Like a Woman.* Do you think any man would read it? I seriously doubt it. Men don't buy books like that; only we do. We are all still stuck on trying to win a man's approval, his validation, and his affections, whereas men just go along and let life happen. Men don't fear being themselves. Men don't worry that to pursue a career is to lose love or the chance at family. Yet we do worry about these issues. In fact, we are obsessed by it. Our socialization runs thousands of years deep. In some places in the world (such as in parts of the Middle East and Africa) women are still considered the property of their husbands and treated as less than chattel. They are uneducated, impoverished, and often beaten, raped, or sold off into the sex slave trade—lest we forget the tragic kidnapping of over two hundred Nigerian schoolgirls by Islamic extremist Boko Haram in April 2014. Many believe the girls were sold into marriage or slavery for $12 each.[2]

Yes, women are still being treated in many parts of the world as subhuman beings. It's as if most of the world is still stuck in the eighteenth century, while more modernized countries like the USA, Canada, the UK, and Germany have empowered women to lead, govern, and run big companies, universities, and foundations. But how far have we really come in the Western world when in our minds we still feel like we have to be like one of the guys and embrace "guy traits" to be accepted and promoted through the corporate or industry ranks?

In this Code we are going to dissect some of these questions. I want to offer you two keys for how to unlock your career aspirations and goals in life, *not by thinking like a man* but instead *learning from them*. I think we can learn a lot from successful men while keeping our femininity and our uniqueness as women intact. Here are the keys we will explore:

1. It is something special to be a woman.
2. We can learn from men without thinking or acting like them.

It Is Something Special to Be a Woman

What makes women tick? How do we love, laugh, and live? What is it about us, about our very essence, that can bring a grown man to his knees, change the mood of an entire room just by entering it, or with the very warmth of our touch and words change the mind and soul of the most hardened of politicians? I suspect no one knows the answers to the mysteries of being a woman, because no two women are the same. Yet we are very connected as women by these universal truths:

- No matter our culture or geographical location, we are taught to be second to our male counterparts.

- No matter our ethnicity or religion, we are taught to be nurturers, caretakers, and service-minded to others.

- No matter when we are born, or of what station, all women face universal stereotypes and limitations placed on us by male-dominated power structures and institutions.

In order for this to change, we are going to have to redefine what it means to be a woman and what we want as women. This must start when we are girls. This year the Girl Scouts of America and Sheryl Sandberg's Lean In nonprofit organization started a campaign to ban the word *bossy*. The movement called "Ban Bossy" comes from the age-old phrase every girl heard growing up if she took charge, dared to speak up, or showed any leadership traits reserved for boys: "She's bossy." It's the small definitions that shape us in life. Key words used by others to tell us who we are and who we should not become as women.

Is it any wonder, then, that we are constantly being given advice by men on how to better manage ourselves around them and constantly being told that something is wrong with the way we feel and the way we act, and how we think, view the world, love, lead, and live life? We readily take advice from a man but will reject the same wisdom from a woman. That has to change. The time has come for us to embrace what being a "woman" is all about. It is strength, grace, compassion, wisdom, discernment, loyalty, patience, intelligence, ingenuity, empathy, courage, faith, honor, creativity, peace, leadership, power, sisterhood, faithfulness, resilience, and love.

Being a woman does not mean that we have to have a career or work outside the home to embrace and understand what amazingly fabulous creatures we are and how powerful we are by the sheer force of our femininity, mystery, intelligence, and grace. We should not shrink from being all woman. Nor do we need to prove how "tough" we can be in our climb up the corporate ladder and through the ranks of management, government, academia, industry, and even the military. We ascend because we are capable, qualified, and gifted, not because we have to be like men.

Let me disabuse you of this notion. Acting like a man, or even thinking like one, is not only a *career limiting move* in all of the cases I have ever seen as a professional woman, but it also has unintended spillover into your personal life. It can create havoc in your interpersonal and dating relationships. Once you turn something on, it is hard to turn it off. You can't be one woman at work and another woman at home. You have to be YOU. Whoever *you* is.

A woman has to show up in the world. She has to share her gifts with the world. She has to be willing to stand on her principles. And she has to be willing to dare to be the woman of her dreams. The key to getting what we want from our careers is not to be like men or to think like them; the key is to unlock the woman who resides inside us, with all her splendor, intellect, and bravery, and let her show up ready every day in the world.

You have to know your value, and you have to know your worth. It all starts there. If you don't see what you bring to the table, no one else ever will. The truth is, women and men are very different for a reason. It's called balance. We were never designed to be the same. Just watch boys and girls at play. Very different. Watch men and women at work. Very different. Everything about what we do as men and women is just, well, different.

> You have to know your value, and you have to know your worth. It all starts there.

For example, I read about a fascinating study conducted by researchers at the University of Pennsylvania, where they attempted to better understand the differences between the brains of men and women.[3] To do so, scientists scanned the brains of 949 young men and women in the biggest investigation of its kind thus far. What they found is something we as women have known for centuries: the female brain is hardwired to be better at multitasking, while men are better at concentrating on single, complex activities. "Using 'hi-tech diffusion MRI imaging,' scientists mapped the connections between different parts of the brain and discovered that women have much better connections between the left and right sides of the brain. However, men showed more activity within the brain's individual parts, particularly in the cerebellum, the part of the brain that controls motor skills."[4]

My point is this: our very anatomy and our "wiring" as women is not just to be better multitaskers, which we are, but to be better at nurturing, supporting, and caring, which we are. I think this combination of innate Code skills is something that we need to start using to our career advantage. As leaders of a new generation of women, in an age of innovation, technology, and science, we are hardwired for success. This new age calls for multitasking excellence, life integration, emotional intelligence (see Code 14), the ability to manage three different generations in the workforce all at once (Baby Boomer, Gen X, and Gen Y), and most important the ability to lead from within our Code versus looking at male-dominated models of leadership.

Let's face it: the women we most admire in history and in modern times all have one big thing in common—they broke the rules. They shattered glass ceilings, chiseled through brick walls, and took everything that was thrown at them and made it work for them. That is what being a woman is all about.

We Can Learn from Men without Thinking or Acting Like Them

In my more than twenty years of being a professional woman (first as a young attorney and committee counsel on Capitol Hill and later as a White House reporter/TV pundit), I have had several powerful male mentors. I have learned a lot from these men of influence and power. I still have lunch regularly with one of my male mentors, whom I met when I was twenty-four years old. I was a clerk at his law firm in Washington, DC, and we have been connected ever since.

I call him whenever I need to make big professional decisions. I can bounce things off him, and he will always give it to me straight. I learned early in my career life to surround myself with mentors and sponsors who had achieved the success I wanted to achieve in the fields in which I wanted to achieve that success. I listened to these men, and I watched them negotiate deals, manage conflict, and thrive not just in their careers but as husbands, fathers, and sons. And it is true that men handle things very differently than we do. Not better; just differently.

Here is some of what I learned and some of what I hope will help you as a woman in your professional and career life. Even if you are not currently working, are still in school, or have taken a life "off ramp" to raise your family, these ten tips can help you—as they have me—learn from smart, successful, and caring men, yet not feel like you have to be like them.

1. Be a woman. Never feel like you have to act like a man. If you do so, men will not respect you and women will not like you. Be you. Remember what men said about women in Code 8 (Age Gracefully): they find a woman who knows herself and is comfortable in her own skin powerful and attractive all at once.

2. Ask questions. No question is ever dumb. Being intellectually curious is a good trait. Men never apologize for anything they say, do, or ask.

3. Speak up for yourself. If you don't, we cannot hear your voice.

4. Ask for what you want.

5. Surround yourself with smart people.

6. Cut to the chase. Go for what you want in life. Be competitive, but be willing to collaborate to get what you want. Having 50 percent of the pie is better than 100 percent of no pie. (My Nana told me that.)

7. Fight fair. Shake hands when it is over. No grudge holding.

8. Say thank you.

9. Follow your instincts.
10. Most of all, have a thick hide, or tough skin. Do not take criticism or negative feedback personally. Learn from it.

These are just a few of the things I have learned at the table with men of power. But I think there is more we can learn from men. We need to use our connections and relationships with all the men in our lives as classrooms for learning. Our relationships with men can serve as a powerful mirror that reflects the qualities we have long desired in order to become more successful, balanced, whole, and authentic. Think back to what I said at the outset of this chapter: boys and girls are different. Men and women are likewise very different. And the reason for it is because we balance each other out. We can learn from men, just as they can and should learn from us as leaders and managers in the workplace. When both genders are fully empowered to be themselves, we will see a shift in the work environment and how people learn to lead from within.

Living the Code

At the end of the day, things will only change for women seeking to break the proverbial glass ceiling when we fully embrace our value. Such a change will not come easily. But it is coming. You can see it in movements, organizations, and partnerships forming with women around the world to enhance, develop, and build up other women. Women are beginning to understand that we have to start with our girls. We have to stop allowing them to be labeled "bossy" and teach them the skills necessary to grow up and become bosses if that is what they choose.

The operative word is *choice*. That is what being a woman is all about: the power to choose what we want, who we want to be, and how we want to do it. The power of being a woman never rests in acting like or trying to think like a man. We should respect men and the virtues and strengths they possess, as well as those we possess. This is not complicated stuff, Sisters of the Code. It's simply time for us to stand up and be heard.

Key Words

Woman	Definitions	Independence
Man	Respect	Learning
Freedom	Value	
Labels	Conformity	

Code
14

Lead from Within

If your emotional abilities aren't in hand, if you don't have self-awareness, if you are not able to manage your distressing emotions, if you can't have empathy and have effective relationships, then no matter how smart you are, you are not going to get very far.

—Daniel Goleman

Leading from within is another way of saying "emotional intelligence." We as women are, in my humble opinion, naturally emotionally intelligent. We are kind. We are empathetic. We are great multitaskers. But we also can be hardest on ourselves and on one another. I wanted to do a Code about the power of harnessing our emotions and using it as a tool to choose how we think, feel, and act. It shapes our interactions with others and our understanding of ourselves. It defines how and what we learn; it allows us to set priorities; it determines the majority of our daily actions. Research suggests it is responsible for as much as 80 percent of the "success" in our lives. Simply put, emotional intelligence is the ability to lead from your heart. It is the ability to detect strengths and weaknesses in those around you and those who work with and for you. It is to be perceptive of their dreams, goals, and aspirations. But most importantly, it is to be emotionally connected in a professional setting.

The truth is, we don't talk much anymore. We text, instant message, direct message, or email. Lost is the precious art of direct, courageous, and compassionate conversation that makes Code 19 (Have Courageous Conversations) so transformative and essential for our lives as women bosses, business owners, academics, researchers, and executives. It's as if we celebrate being distant and disconnected. We like our walls. Whether in the workplace or in business, we want to do everything according to what the numbers say, what the profit margin is, and what the computer analysis tells us to do. We view every decision through the lens of our own professional "advancement," and as such we view caring for those we work with and for as somewhat of a weakness. In reality, this caring is our greatest strength in the context of emotional intelligence and career advancement.

As a new generation of leaders, we think showing empathy and compassion makes us seem soft. Women have been brainwashed to think that we have to be tough and blunt like men. That we have to think and act like men or we will not move ahead. Truth be told, we like that there are layers between us and other people that didn't exist before the advent of technology. We can hide behind an electronic memo or group email. The people who work for us may never see our faces. It's not necessary, particularly in big companies and global corporations. We are masters of "distraction." We are beholden to "busy." And we have little time (or so we think) to deal with people, their problems, and their purpose.

Yet, not doing so misses a new kind of leadership and business engagement model that is required for our time. I call it **Focused. Fair. Flexible.** The new kind of female leader is a woman who operates by a Code.

> The new kind of female leader is a woman who operates by a Code.

Sure, she is smart, curious, creative, loyal, educated, and committed. But beyond that she knows how and when to use her heart to lead from a deep place within. From her Code of self-value, resiliency, personal accountability, teaching people how to treat her, and having made peace with her past, this woman leader knows how to treat people as she wants to be treated. And in so doing, she wins the loyalty, respect, admiration, and love of all who know her.

This new kind of power woman "career girl" takes care of herself. She doesn't run herself ragged because she is centered in what truly matters in life. She understands that work is what we do, not who we are. More than that, she is compassionate. She has a heart for other women (and men). She understands the plight of single moms, working moms, and women caring for aging parents. She knows that flexibility is a key component of twenty-first-century leadership.

Today, women stay single longer, have children later in life, and make up over 50 percent of the workforce in America and over 30 percent globally. The statistics paint a clear picture of who we are as women and what we will need to succeed. According to the Shriver Report, founded by Maria Shriver, working mothers are struggling to make ends meet. More than 42 million women in the USA live in poverty, with millions more on the "brink" of poverty:

> The reality is that a third of all American women are living *at or near a space we call* "the brink of poverty." We define this as less than 200 percent of the federal poverty line, or about $47,000 per year for a family of four. Forty-two million women, and the 28 million children who depend on them, are living one single incident—a doctor's bill, a late paycheck, or a broken-down car—away from economic ruin. Women make up nearly two-thirds of minimum-wage workers, the vast majority of whom receive no paid sick days. This is at a time when women earn most of the college and advanced degrees in this country, make most of the consumer spending decisions by far, and are more than half of the nation's voters.[1]

Women need other women. Long gone are the days when companies paid their workers hefty pensions or retirement benefits beyond a 401(k). Long gone are the days when workers stayed at the same company for thirty or more years. And long gone are the days when men were the sole wage earners and women could stay home with their children. Most women must work.

The average female worker today stays at her job 4.4 years, according to the Bureau of Labor Statistics, and female Millennials may change jobs up to ten times in their lifetime.[2] This means that today's female managers, leaders, and workers will need an extra handle on human capital management and relationships. Smart companies will want to not only attract top female talent out of colleges and industry, but they will also want to retain and advance those women as they come up through the ranks. Hence, the ability to express and control our own emotions as leaders is important, but so is our ability to understand, interpret, and respond to the emotions of others. Emotional intelligence (EI) refers to the ability to perceive, control, and evaluate emotions.

The best leaders usually have something beyond their behavior—something distinctive—that commands attention, wins people's trust, and enables them to lead successfully. This "something" is often called "leadership presence," which comes from a theory developed by James Scouller, author of *The Three Levels of Leadership: How to Develop Your Leadership Presence, Knowhow and Skill.*

In this Code, we are going to look at three leadership characteristics you can use to build trust: (1) the ability to remain focused and to deal with distractions, (2) the ability to be fair with yourself and others, and (3) the ability to be flexible. Above all, I believe that flexibility is the glue that keeps life, living, and loving intact. These three traits are only a few of what makes up the full spectrum of emotional intelligence, but of all the traits, I think these three are the most simple and the most overlooked. Scientists and researchers tend to focus on "empathy" being the most important. I would agree. However, if you can master these three traits, you will be practicing the art of empathy in spades. And it will yield amazing dividends both professionally and personally.

One of the things we need most as a nation and as a global community is for women to become more active in the political and judicial arenas. As we have seen, women who get involved in politics and hold high offices are rarely involved in sex scandals or ethics probes. We can also note that women who lead countries tend to implement programs and policies that unite leaders, help the poor, care for children, and lift people higher. **Bottom line:**

women bring something compassionate and crucial to the arena of politics and leadership that is sorely missing in our time. We bring the Code of what it means to live life on many levels. We are life integrators because we are master multitaskers, listeners, collaborators, implementers, and fixers all at once.

This Code has three keys:

1. Be focused.
2. Be fair.
3. Be flexible.

Be Focused

A great African proverb says, "The lion does not turn around when a small dog barks." That proverb is pure power because it means that you have to pay attention to what you give your attention to. The enemy of focus is distraction. And today, distractions meet us around every corner. Distractions are those things (or people) that prevent someone from giving full attention to something else. A distraction can be an agitation. An inconvenience. An emergency. A personal demand. Whatever "it" is, distractions take us out of our power, and they take us out of focus. Distractions can disrupt your destiny.

> A great African proverb says, "The lion does not turn around when a small dog barks."

Any good leader, manager, or CEO will tell you that you must maximize the gift of focus. Being able to focus is what builds successful businesses, organizations, and teams. To focus is to have a vision, to have an intention, and to have a way to make that vision, dream, or desired outcome possible. To focus is to make decisions and to execute those decisions well and intentionally.

We never have enough time. Time is our most precious commodity. The only way to preserve and maximize our time, then, is to be focused. Here are five great tips for avoiding distractions and staying focused in your professional and personal life:

1. If you have a goal, a mission, a desire, focus intently on that thing.
2. Quickly get rid of anything that does not align with or get you to your focused goal or mission. It's a distraction.
3. Have a checklist of three things you must do each day. Must do. And then do them. Everything else is extra and can wait.
4. Minimize contacts with people who are "distracters." You know the ones; they are emotional, draining, talkers, and time stealers. They are that small barking dog. You are a lion. Stay focused.
5. Guard your mind and energy space. Make it a place that no one can interrupt. You have the power to decide who gets access to you and who does not. Period.

Be Fair

The second key to unlocking your leadership potential is to practice the skill of being "fair." Now "fair" can be a subjective term. What is fair to me may not be at all fair to you. But at its core, to be fair means to be considerate, legitimate, balanced, flexible (we will address that next), and honest. It can also mean to extend grace. Practicing fairness as a virtue in life, then, is critical. All of us need fairness. We all need grace. Being fair is a vital team-building tool. As women, one of our greatest strengths is that we learn quickly how to share and manage our decisions in ways that best meet the needs of all parties.

Being fair is a key that unlocks creativity, confidence, and courage in your workforce and in your efforts to build teams in enterprise, the church, corporate environments, academia, industry, or any setting you so choose. Fairness matters. Let's break down what fairness looks like and you can begin to implement it into your day-to-day routines.

As a former corporate attorney, I can tell you that most complaints in the workplace come from three areas: (1) pay systems/benefits, (2) managerial favoritism, and (3) equal recognition/treatment. We also know that most women and women of color either lose their jobs or quit their jobs not because they are "incompetent" or "unqualified" but because they were unable to manage personality and conflict style issues in a way that left them (or their bosses) feeling heard and validated.

Here are some things I have learned as a senior counsel in a big law firm and as a committee counsel on Capitol Hill:

1. Fairness is more than a set of rules and handbook procedures.
2. Fairness is an atmosphere. It is a human connectivity that encourages others to speak up, be authentic, and thrive at what they do.
3. Treat people as you want to be treated. Good leaders are great people managers. They like people, they understand the layers of human emotion, and they understand the importance of being fair.
4. Solicit feedback regularly from your team, managers, sales force, and superiors about how you are doing, how you can improve, and what you can learn. This makes people feel engaged, that they have a "say" in what goes on. This creates a sense of fairness that leads to a more open work environment.
5. Make people feel safe and secure. Fairness creates security. And it is important that people who work with you, for you, or around you feel a sense of permanency and security, that they feel you have created a safe working environment in which they can thrive.

Be Flexible

To be flexible is to be able to run the world. My grandmother taught me that. Flexibility is the "glue" that holds our relationships together. Whether with our spouse, kids, parents, siblings, or best friends, when we are flexible we bring out the best in others and ourselves. We allow for spontaneity, creativity, honesty, and a feeling of security. If the people who work with you know you are flexible, they also know they can be honest with you. They know you are a person who seeks solutions. And they know you are a person who can be trusted to do what is best for everyone involved to the best of your ability.

Flexibility is a way of turning the Golden Rule (treat others as you want to be treated) on its head. A better way to think of practicing flexibility in leadership is to stop treating others the way *you* want to be treated and treat them the way *they* want to be treated. Our ability to be flexible (i.e., to be capable of bending without breaking) unlocks greater partnerships, deeper relationships, and more connected team leadership development at work. Leadership models of flexibility (or as it is sometimes called, "situational leadership") suggest that the type of leadership a leader adopts should reflect the context in which she finds herself. In this model, a leader considers the nature of her task, the culture and objectives of the organization, the people and resources available, and the general environment when selecting her approach to leadership. This allows for maximum flexibility and adaptability, while still being able to lead as she desires. Let's break down how flexibility looks, operates, and benefits both the leader and those being led.

- **Understand your own natural style.** Your leadership style is distinct because you are distinct. Learn how you lead, how you delegate, how you encourage, how you discipline. And evaluate how you respond and listen to feedback as well as provide feedback. Your style will teach your team and colleagues how to respond to you, approach you, or not approach you.
- **Notice the styles of others.** This is critical to being fair and flexible. Are your team members outgoing, talkative, quiet?

Do they like to socialize outside of work? What are they like under stress? A great book to read on this subject is *People Styles at Work . . . and Beyond: Making Bad Relationships Good and Good Relationships Better* by Robert Bolton and Dorothy Grover Bolton. You can even have your teams take the simple assessment in the Boltons' book and talk about how to use the results to improve working relationships and communication.

- **Acknowledge style differences and work to meet halfway.** When you are working with people with different styles from your own, let them know that your preferences are different but that you will work to meet them closer to their comfort zone. In turn, you would like them to shift to meet you part-way. Communication upfront reduces negative judgments of other styles and makes this issue something you can work on together. It is all about communicating that you are "open" to being flexible.

Bottom line: becoming a more flexible leader makes you a more powerful leader. The greatest leaders can shift their behavior to create results, rather than staying stuck in their own behavioral box.

Living the Code

We are all creatures of habit. Practicing a Code of focus, fairness, and flexibility helps us to grow as leaders and helps us to build other women leaders along the way.

Classic emotional intelligence (Emotional IQ) theory suggests that there are four branches of emotional intelligence: the perception of emotions, the ability to reason using emotions, the ability to understand emotions, and the ability to manage emotions.

1. **Perceiving emotions:** The first step in understanding emotions is to accurately perceive them. In many cases, this might involve understanding nonverbal signals such as body language and facial expressions. Perception is often reality. So if you are using perception, you have to be sure to get some facts to go along with it so that it is based in reality.

2. **Reasoning with emotions:** The next step involves using emotions to promote thinking and cognitive activity. Emotions help prioritize what we pay attention and react to; we respond emotionally to things that garner our attention or interest.

3. **Understanding emotions:** The emotions or actions we perceive can carry a wide variety of meanings. That is why taking the time to ask questions and gain clarity matters most. If someone expresses angry emotions, for example, we as the observer must interpret the cause of their anger and what it might mean. For example, if your boss is acting angry, it might mean that he is dissatisfied with your work, or it could be because he got a speeding ticket on his way to work that morning or that he's been fighting with his wife. Ask questions; get information. That allows you to properly assess and understand.

4. **Managing emotions:** The ability to manage your emotions effectively is a key part of emotional intelligence. Regulating emotions, responding appropriately, and responding to the emotions of others are all important aspects of emotional management. Good leaders do this well. They get it—because they know how to focus, be fair, and be flexible.

🔑 Key Words

Empathy	Focus	Shift
Intellect	Flexibility	Open
Connection	Distraction	Communication
Emotion	Fairness	Team
Intelligence	Interest	
Compassion	Manage	

Be Brave

I want to be in the arena. I want to be brave with my life. And when
we make the choice to dare greatly, we sign up to get our asses
kicked. We can choose courage, or we can choose comfort, but we
cannot have both. Not at the same time.

—Brené Brown

Bravery. What a word. It means so many things. And it can come
to us and be lived out by us in so many different forms. When
I think of the brave women in my life, they all have one thing in
common: courage. You see, bravery and courage go hand in hand.
One is the act of being honest with yourself, and summoning the
guts to be willing to do what you are afraid to do. The other is
the steps that you take to walk that courage out. Every day of our
lives as women—no matter where we come from, what we do for
a living, or our level of education—requires us to pull from a deep
well. A sacred space. A place that defies our emotions and forces
us to do what we must do.

Your dreams, ambitions, and deepest desires come with a price.

Your dreams will demand that you summon untapped courage. Being a woman who wants to make a difference, change the
conversation, and be a leader is not easy. You are required to go
against the grain and be willing to stand alone. You will work long
hours at great personal sacrifice. Standing in the arena and battling
back will test you. It will shake you. But most of all it will require
that you be *brave*.

Yes, I said *brave.*

Not courageous, not bold, not persevering (although you must be that), but *brave.* You see bravery is different from these virtues. Bravery is something you do when everything inside of you says it cannot be done, should not be done, or has never been done before. Bravery is not what you talk about, think about, or wonder about. Bravery is what **you do.** Bravery is what you live. Bravery is defiance in the face of demand. Bravery says, *No matter where I find myself in life, it is not too late to live the life of my dreams.*

Bravery is freedom. Bravery is peace. Bravery is bigger than courage. Bravery makes us bold. It summons something deep within us; it pulls us to purpose. Bravery is a commanding of the spirit. Bravery is what every woman needs to pursue her passion. Never let anyone tell you anything different. Sadly, all of our lives as women (at least the vast majority of us) we have been told that we shouldn't be too much of this or too little of that. That we shouldn't be "bossy." That we should never be perceived as being too "aggressive" or too "independent" and that we should put the needs and wants of others first.

> Bravery is freedom.
> Bravery is peace.
> Bravery is bigger
> than courage.
> Bravery makes us
> bold. It summons
> something deep
> within us; it pulls us
> to purpose. Bravery
> is a commanding of
> the spirit.

This programming is hard to overcome. It is embedded in us as little girls and continues throughout our lives. It causes us deep conflict as we wrestle against our dreams, our desires, and our adventurous spirits, and weigh them against the call of our hearts to be wives, mothers, and caretakers. I could not disagree more with writers who summarize a "woman's heart" as being only interested in fairy tales, romance, and castles. The fairy tale books got it wrong. We are not princesses hiding in the tower in the kingdom, waiting to be rescued by a prince on a white horse.

It's simply not true.

Like our male counterparts, we, too, want to explore, create, build, and discover new worlds. To be brave is to admit this truth to ourselves and do whatever it is we want to do. If we are going to begin to live out our dreams and aspirations, then we must shift away from old stereotypes and move to a new frontier of womanhood, one that empowers us to be able to pursue the lives we want without feeling guilty, without feeling overwhelmed, and without feeling like we left someone or something behind.

Life requires us to make brave choices. While we hide behind a composed facade, most of us are fragile. In the face of adversity, we become fearful and inhibited by what others might think. Then we freeze. And our wings dip instead of lifting us higher. When we learn to be brave, we keep going in spite of the perceived risks. If we lack bravery, key opportunities will pass us by and the world will crush our spirits with its customary indifference. Worry is the enemy of purpose. To worry is to fear, and to fear is to lose your faith.

Successful women know how to navigate the nagging voices of doubt that can so easily discourage them from making the brave choices of living. To give in to doubt once can become habitual and rob us of our true power. But bravery calls us to act. To have courage is to make a decision. To follow through on that courage you have deep within is to free yourself to be authentically and completely who God gifted you to be.

In this Code we are going to unlock three keys of bravery that will help you in your professional and personal life.

1. Master your fear.
2. Summon your courage.
3. Go confidently toward your dreams.

Let's face it: *bravery* is not a word we use much as women. We associate bravery with men, with heroes in battle. But we do ourselves a great disservice to only associate men with bravery because women are the bravest beings to ever live. Women have been a part of every story, family, crusade, battle, war, revolution, and transformation in history.

We need to celebrate bravery as part of who we are as women. We need to celebrate women who are brave. Every day women work to make ends meet, working double shifts and supplementing their husbands' incomes to lift their families. Women take care of aging parents, encourage friends, start charities, take care of our homes, and foster children. We do these things from love, but the bravery to forge ahead gets it all done.

Master Your Fear

Fear is one of life's constant companions. As Mark Twain once said, "Courage is resistance to fear, mastery of fear—not absence of fear."[1] So let's talk about fear.

First, fear is normal. It is good to be afraid. It is our mind's way of telling us that we should be aware of danger. Think about it. You don't fear everything. It is usually the big decisions, the big goals, the big life choices that make us most afraid. Fear, then, is something we have to learn to embrace so that we can make a decision. The most important thing to remember about fear is NOT to let it paralyze you.

I keep journals. When I turned forty I reread those journals. I found a pattern in my writings that astonished me: I wrote a lot about my fears. What if this? Or what if that? As I look back, almost everything I wanted to do has come true, except for the two most important things in my life: marriage and children. Stuff happens. Life happens. Sometimes we let things wound us so deeply that we become afraid to love again. To try again. And we lose time.

While fear is normal, fear is not your friend. Fear sets off a chain of emotions that can cause us to miss open doors and better opportunities. It all comes down to how we master our fear. Being afraid is normal, but you can learn to master it and run against it.

I am old school, and I like lists. Taking out pen and paper and writing something out has great practical and emotional benefits. Here is my checklist for facing and fighting your fears:

- **Face it.** What am I really afraid of? Is it failure or success? Many people miss the latter part of this question. Sometimes we don't fear that we won't succeed; we fear that we will. And if we do, what does that mean to our current life situation, status, and comfort? You have to face the thing you fear so that you can conquer it. You cannot fix what you will not face.

- **Check your comfort zone and get out of the box.** Comfort is the enemy of courage. Comfort and contentment are not the same. You can be content and still see roads and new paths ahead. But when you get comfortable, you can get stuck. To be brave means to step outside your "box." One of the worst things we do is to allow others to define our capabilities and possibilities and then live in the box they create for us. It's time to get out of your box. Being safe is the enemy of getting satisfied.

- **Make a decision.** You can never face your fears unless you grasp the power of making decisions. Just choose. And go for it. Don't let the past make you fearful. Experience is a great teacher. But experience can also work hand in hand with fear. Experience will tell you: You can't do that. You are too old. You are too young. You are not smart enough. Bad experiences teach us to be fearful of what good can lie ahead. Don't make passive decisions by not deciding in life. If there is an open door, a new opportunity, a new job, a chance to start your own business, make a list of pros and cons, talk to your support circle or family, and then decide. But decide on the facts, not on your fears.

- **Accept that failure is an option.** Acceptance is a powerful key for life. When we accept, we can go forward. It is better to try and to fail than to never try. Some of our greatest leaders, explorers, and inventors failed time and time again. But they persevered. They kept trying until they finally succeeded or had to walk a different path. As Thomas Edison once said when asked how he came up with the light bulb, "I have not failed. I've just found 10,000 ways that won't work." My point is, try it. Yes, failure can happen. But don't dwell there. Learn to dwell in what is possible and new in your life.

- **Now go do.** The way I have overcome my greatest fears is to take a deep breath and, after having done all of the above, to just jump. To take the risk. To execute the plan. Women can be risk averse whereas our male counterparts are not. We like safety and security by nature because we have been socialized that way. There comes a time when you must throw off those things that easily entangle you and run with the wind. Take a risk and learn how to fly. It is never too late to begin again. Never. But you have to be willing to jump.

Summon Your Courage

Courage is the attitude; bravery is the action. Courage is the voice inside that says, "I think I can." Bravery goes out and proves that you can. Courage is different from bravery. Courage precedes bravery. Courage is the ability to face difficulty, danger, stress, or pain. Having courage does not mean you will not be afraid. You will be. Courage, as someone once said, is "fear that has said its prayers." Courage is what propels you and gives you the ability to be brave. To make it happen. Courage tells you that you CAN.

Bravery and courage are twin siblings, but they are not identical twins. They are fraternal twins. They hold hands. They whisper to one another. They need one another. So whether you are deciding to reenter the workforce after being a stay-at-home mom or you are twenty-five and deciding to travel halfway around the world for that great new job, you must summon the priceless virtue of courage that rests inside of you. We all have it. *Courage*, like *bravery*, is not a word we associate with womanhood because we believe it is a masculine word, a word reserved for men in battle or in business. Sisters of the Code, we must dare to find the courage that lies within so that we can tap into the bravery that allows us to go and do.

Courage is what shows up in the midst of the storms. Courage is what shows up when we lose our job. Courage is what shows up when our spouse loses his job. Courage is what shows up when our child gets sick with cancer or our mom suffers a stroke. Courage is what happens when we lose all we have but give thanks for what we still have left. Courage is what happens when you sit in the meeting and the boss turns to you and says, "What do you think?" Courage is a part of our everyday lives as women. It is that thing inside us that pushes us to step up, grow up, get up, and go meet our friend bravery on the battlefield of life. Here are my five keys to unlocking the courage inside of you:

1. **You must have a strong spiritual life.** Your courage is in direct proportion to your prayer, meditation, and spiritual center. Now, let me be clear. There will be moments in your life that shake you to your core. You will lose your way. You may question your faith. But if you have a strong spiritual foundation and center, you will find your way back. You will be resilient. You will be brave.

2. **You must have a strong front row of friends and supporters.** Code 17 (Know Your Front Row) is all about who you have around you in this life. Your courage will be connected to who speaks into your life and supports and encourages you.

3. **You must know yourself.** This goes back to Code 1 (Know Your Value). You must trust yourself. You must be willing to stand in the arena of life, bloodied but not bowed. You must be willing to go against your family, your friends, and your fears in order to get to the goal.

4. **You must believe in yourself.** Even if no one else in the world believes in you, you must believe in you. Period.

5. **You must be resilient.** Code 7 (Be Resilient) is probably my greatest Code of success in life. I have been knocked down, knocked around, beaten down. But I keep getting back up

again. The ability to be resilient is huge. Everyone depends on us. So we must be able to depend on ourselves. Keep getting back up no matter what life does to you.

These five keys, no matter who you are or where you find yourself, are essential to having the life you desire professionally, personally, and relationally.

Go Confidently toward Your Dreams

Fear is met by courage on the way to confidence. To be confident is to harness the most amazing transformative power there is in life. Confidence is power. Confidence is belief. Confidence is awareness. Confidence is acceptance. Confidence is what we have when we have made a decision and put that decision into practice.

Your level of self-confidence shows up in many ways: your behavior, your body language, how you speak, what you say, and so on. The most important trait we need to instill in our daughters, nieces, and younger sisters is confidence. It forms the center of all we want to become in life. Confidence pushes us to be brave. It propels us to go against the grain. It is the small voice that whispers, "You can do this." Boys are taught to be confident, to take control, and to win at life. Girls, not so much. By the time we reach our forties and fifties, we usually begin to suffer a confidence erosion because of our age, others' expectations, and the pressures of life. We begin to listen to the "tapes" we play in our heads about what we no longer can do. We need to listen to freeing tapes that say, "I can."

Confidence is something we have to practice. And like anything we practice, we get better over time. You will not be confident in all things in life. And that is okay. I could never climb Mount Everest because I am afraid of extreme heights. I have no desire to climb that mountain. Confidence is also *knowing our limitations* in life. It allows us to confidently say NO to things that are not for us. Confidence gives you the power, that centering, and that push to be able to define and redefine your life at any stage. Here are some steps you can take to build confidence in your life:

- **Know yourself.** There it is again. To know yourself, who you are, what you need, and what you want is the gravity of your universe. You must have good self-esteem to be confident. You cannot have confidence if you don't think you are worthy, deserving, or capable of doing something.

- **Be prepared.** This is huge. Preparation is everything. There are no shortcuts. You have to do the work, put in the time, learn the language, know the pitfalls, trust your intellect, follow your heart, and practice your craft. Preparation allows us to be brave on the battlefield.

- **Be coachable.** Feedback from other trusted sources, mentors, teachers, family, and friends is crucial to your life success. You will build your confidence by taking wise counsel, by accepting correction, and by being coachable.

Living the Code

Mastery of fear + courage = confidence. Bravery must have these three virtues in alignment to succeed. Your ability to move forward and to do more with your life comes from within. Bravery cannot be taught. Bravery must be summoned from deep within your soul.

Key Words

Bravery	Control	Instinct
Courage	Boldness	Experience
Confidence	Redefining	Awareness
Fear	Coachable	

Code 16

Lift Other Women
as You Climb

> Women who understand how powerful they are do not give in to
> envy over meaningless things, instead they fight to maintain the
> beautiful bond of the sisterhood. These are the real women who
> know that we need each other's love and support to survive in this
> world. Love is the essence of being a woman. We must be that light
> of love that seals the bond and unique beauty of our sisterhood.
> —Bindu Maira, motivational speaker

After Code #1: Know Your Value, this is the Code that is sacrosanct, emblematic of what it means to be a woman and to honor other women. I could not have made it this far in my life without other women along my journey correcting me, challenging me, pushing me, lifting me, and most of all loving me. We are sisters interlocked in a cosmic dance of space and time. We can be so much when we lift each other up. And we can be so small when we tear one another down. But it all comes down to honoring the "sisterhood of women."

Sisterhood. What a word of contradictions.

How is it possible to be so connected to someone who is not your biological relation, yet who knows you better than you know yourself? The women we embrace as our "sisters" are sometimes closer than our own family members. They defend us, wipe away our tears, take care of us when we are ill, let us bunk in their homes, watch our kids, pray with us, push us, pull us, and passionately support our dreams. At the same time, these same women will not hesitate to scold us, check us, and even anger us in order to protect us.

True sisterhood, however, cannot be forced. It has to be developed over time. Not every woman will be your best friend, nor should she be invited to be in your inner circle, but every woman is deserving of your respect and support if only in the form of a smile. *Sisterhood* is not a trite word. Being your sister's keeper should *be a reflex*. It should be based on how you would want to be treated if you were walking in her shoes. Sisterhood knows no boundary, no race, no class or geography. Sisterhood transcends and it transforms us for the better. Sisterhood is from the heart.

> True sisterhood, however, cannot be forced. It has to be developed over time. Not every woman will be your best friend, nor should she be invited to be in your inner circle, but every woman is deserving of your respect and support if only in the form of a smile.

Being a woman is all about being with other women. It starts when we are little girls passing notes in school or asking the girl in the row next to us if she will be our best friend. We remember nights in our sleeping bags, giggling and talking about boys at slumber parties. We learned early that other girls (who will grow up to be other women) are both our competition and our coconspirators. Therein lies our conflict.

Yet, deep inside we know that we are at our best when we have our sisters (biological or not) at our side, cheering us on and watching our backs.[1] As women, we are not just *connected*, we are *interconnected*. So why does it seem that at a time when so many of us are getting ahead and doing amazing things that far too many of us are being left behind? The truth is, many women, despite their achievements or power, are just too afraid, too unaware, or too insecure to help other women. And that is what sisterhood is all about—helping each other. Because the reality is this, if we don't help each other, who will? And if not now, when?

Who are we and what do we want from one another? What do we owe one another as women? Things have changed a lot for women in just my lifetime. So I want to challenge you to make one of your most honored Codes a sincere desire to love and support other women. Not just the women in your life, whom you love and who love you. That is easy. I want to challenge all of us to bring other women into

> Being your sister's keeper should *be a reflex*.

our ranks. To help other women out of poverty—whether financial or spiritual. To help other women who are alone in this world. To help other women realize their deepest dreams. Talk is cheap, ladies. What are you doing to lift other women as you climb? In this chapter, we'll examine three keys that will help us to do better as women leading, loving, and caring for other women.

1. What the Sisterhood Code is and why it matters
2. What NOT to do as a leader, friend, or mentor
3. How to become a woman who supports other women

What the Sisterhood Code Is and Why It Matters

We yearn for each other as sisters. We all want to know good women, we all want to be good women, and we all want to raise good women. But somehow we have abandoned ourselves for others' notions of who we are supposed to be. If we are to raise this next generation of women leaders, wives, mothers, and daughters to truly be all they can be, then it starts with the Code, a set of timeless rules that will never change as long as human beings walk the earth.

It is this Code, this set of rules, that drives us to be our best selves, our most authentic selves. And when we can learn to operate in that space of self-love, self-worth, and self-value, we can soar

> We yearn for each other as sisters. We all want to know good women, we all want to be good women, and we all want to raise good women.

to heights unimaginable. We can forge a universal sisterhood so great that we can truly ignite a spark that lights the way and changes the world for all humanity.

In short, it's time for us to put the "sister" back into the word *sisterhood*. It starts with you and with me, right here and right now. The Sisterhood Code requires that we *sharpen one another* as the Scripture so aptly states in Proverbs 27:17. The new model of leadership for women, and frankly, for men, is leading from within. Leading from the heart. Leading with our "soft skills." When we lead from a place of caring, we can all go to the next level. The Code says we "talk before we walk." We sharpen one another by having the courage, empathy, and sisterhood to help another woman if she gets in her own way.

Here is a great example of this principle in action: Oprah Winfrey made award-winning *Fix My Life* star Iyanla Vanzant a household name in the late 1990s. The two parted ways when Iyanla wanted her own show and Oprah counseled, "It's not time yet." Iyanla moved on to get a show of her own that did not work out. Oprah's star continued to rise. Iyanla had hit a rough patch—losing her daughter to cancer, losing her wealth, and struggling to make ends meet. Fast-forward to April 2011. Oprah invited Iyanla back to one of the last *Oprah* shows to discuss her book *Peace from Broken Pieces*, and also to discuss publicly for the first time their very personal falling out.[2] On national TV these two women honored "sisterhood" and talked through their issues with respect, candor, and Code. Here are two key takeaways from their very public conversation (note I did not say texting, emailing, or social media):

1. **Oprah was a sponsor for Iyanla.** Not a mentor but a sponsor. Sponsors use their power and platform to help lift and open doors for other women who have promise and potential.

Oprah often gave her stage to Iyanla and sat in the audience. Iyanla unwisely walked away from her biggest supporter and sponsor. Never walk away from your sponsors. Always exit your relationships well (Code 17). However, once Iyanla fell upon hard times, Oprah chose to love, extend grace, and lift her up. Oprah chose restoration versus gloating.

2. **Iyanla was able to learn the lessons of her pain during her time away from Oprah and return to Oprah humble.** Her ability to admit that she was not in a place to receive all Oprah was giving her in that season was a powerful statement we should all embrace. We have to be whole and healed in order to receive the blessings and the good people that God sends our way. We have to love ourselves first before we can be open to love from others.

If we can learn from these two inspired women, nothing will be impossible for us to conquer. They have taught us that when we can forgive, extend grace, and restore each other when we fall short, what can come out of it is a stronger unity and purpose that helps us to SOAR! What Oprah and Iyanla have modeled for us is a Sister Code of Conduct that says:

- I can handle conflict with other women well.
- I want to pursue peace over being right.
- I can talk to my sister civilly.
- I can hear her point of view and share mine with respect.
- I can have the courage to say *I may be wrong.*
- I can restore my sister because I have been restored.
- I can love her because I have been loved.
- I can forgive her because I have been forgiven.

When we are united as women, we are powerful. We are powerful when we can get beyond our petty squabbles and differences and instead have the courage to listen to one another so that we can heal and grow. You only need look at these two amazing, fabulous women to know that anything is possible when you can operate from a place of love, forgiveness, and restoration.

What NOT to Do as a Leader, Friend, or Mentor

Lynette is a fifty-year-old with a Harvard MBA who left IBM in the early 1990s with three of her colleagues to start an organization called Transform Me. The company's goal was to help the Fortune 100 with diversity and inclusion best practices. Lynette and her peers built a multimillion-dollar business and a coveted annual women's retreat that attracts over one thousand women annually from America's top companies. It is exclusive, expensive, and everyone wants to attend. That is until the last few years.

Lynette has a leadership and personality problem. She does not play well with others. She is controlling. She is abrasive. She offends top executives, talent, and sponsors who come to her event. She feels her brand is worth the price and she will push hard to get what she wants no matter who gets hurt. She has lost faithful supporters because she lacks what I call "soft skills."

Her cofounders are more laid back, and they have allowed her to lead. Lynette is an alpha chick. She gets it done but at a heavy toll on everyone around her. Her peers are afraid of her. They attend the retreat, get what they need, and then sadly talk about her behind her back. No one wants to correct Lynette. This is sad because Lynette has value. She is brilliant. But she is a tyrant. If she could see her way to correction, she could take her organization to a greater level of success.

The Sisterhood Code requires that, if we love our friends, respect our coworkers, and want them to succeed, we speak up in love (admiration) and we offer correction. So clear your space of people who will not love you enough to tell you the truth. Lynette's friends have been remiss. They have allowed her to go unchecked for too long. So Lynette thinks there is no problem. Unfortunately, her two coleads quit the organization and with them went some corporate support. They never talked it out. They got frustrated and walked. Code 19 (Have Courageous Conversations) says we "talk before we walk." We have those courageous conversations. We sharpen one another by having the courage, empathy, and sisterhood to help another woman if she gets in her own way. Because these women have all violated the Code, a long-standing friendship is ruined. A company has lost talent. And women watching the girl drama opted out of something they wanted to support.

Here is another example: Jane married her college sweetheart at twenty-two. She dropped out of college to work so he could attend law school. She's now a mother of three and is headed toward divorce court. She finished her BA at an online college last year, and she wants very much to get back to what she calls the "business of living." Jane has allowed herself to get out of shape, she does not feel great about her life, and she has some minor health issues. Her husband has been engaged in a series of affairs with younger women at his firm, and he makes no secret of the fact that he wants out of his marriage.

Jane is on antidepressants and her friends have quietly removed themselves because they feel she has become toxic. Jane wants to get better. She even wants to save her marriage, but she feels helpless. Jane abandoned herself while focusing on her husband and kids in an unbalanced way.

The Code requires that we take responsibility for our lives and that we make sure that we have a life. We do not put husband and kids so far above self that we forget we have dreams, needs, wants, and desires too. The sisterhood circle also requires that we never abandon our female friends in their time of need. When the dark hours come, we must step up. Jane needs to call her friends and ask for help. She needs to get professional help. She needs to join a weight-loss program, ask her husband to get into marriage counseling, and fight for her life again. Jane needs to know what the Code teaches best: it is never too late to have a life and never too late to change one.

Both of these examples show us what not to do in and among the sisterhood of women. Both Jane and Lynette are good women who lost themselves. Each woman could have been made sharper and more successful had she (a) been coachable and (b) had a good front row of women around her. None of us is an island. We need other people. We need other women to challenge, correct, and be there for us as we must be for them. Sisterhood is a powerful force for change and healing. If we fail to meet another woman where she is, we sow the seeds of neglect in our own lives. It's time we learned how to help each other up and through our most difficult life storms and through our accomplishments.

How to Become a Woman Who Supports Other Women

Life isn't all about you or your success. Or mine. It is about the success of all women. I want to challenge women to make a way for women of the next generation to succeed beyond our wildest dreams. I want to ask you to make a mental pledge to the following when it comes to how you interact with and treat other women.

- **Be kind.** Being a witch (or that other word) to another woman violates the Code. If you are mean or harsh to other women, it will come back to you. Be kind. Be helpful when you can, and if you can't be nice, at least do no harm.

- **Be patient.** You need grace. You need support. You need encouragement. So why won't you give it to another woman who is younger and new at the job, or older and reentering the workforce, or trying to make her way in the world? Treat other women as you WANT to be treated, NOT as you MAY HAVE been treated by bad women on your way up the professional or life ladder. Be a mentor (someone who is a sounding board, guidepost, or seasoned friend) and be a sponsor (someone who is willing to use your access and power to help other women make it).

> Life isn't all about you or your success. Or mine. It is about the success of all women.

- **Communicate.** Talk, do not text. Talk, do not email. Talk, do not gossip. Talk, do not tell your inner circle what she did wrong or how they should avoid her. If you have an issue, go to the woman and talk it out. Stop with the petty schoolgirl antics. And most importantly, stop "going off" on other women. You do irreparable damage to trust and to the sisterhood. If talking does not work, or is not advisable in the situation, the Bible says (for us church girls) that you can take a witness, a mediator, someone who can help you two work it out.

- **Be empathetic.** Empathy is the single most important skill any leader must have. Your ability to relate to, forgive, understand, and engage with other women will impact how successful you are in life, as a leader and as a member of the sisterhood of women. There are no exceptions to this rule. If you cannot find it in your heart to act like a human being before you act like a supervisor, then you have failed at Leadership 101.

- **Operate by a Code of conduct. Don't be a hypocrite.** Do not place yourself above other women just because you have a title, status, or stuff. Just remember that but by chance and God's grace any of us could lose all we have tomorrow: our homes, our families, our good jobs, our health, and our wealth. The next generation of women is watching those of us who are over forty. Reality TV is teaching younger women and some of our peers that being nasty mean girls is the way to succeed in life. *It is not.* We have a responsibility to set an example of what it means to be a "sister" and to "keep" your sister even when we disagree. You cannot live by *do what I* *say, but not what I do.* It will not work with this generation of savvy women. They see you. The question is, do you see you? There is a Code. It's time we lived up to it.

Living the Code

To be a "sister" is to be a friend. To be loyal. Tried-and-true. It is to give a smile, lend a hand, and practice friendship. It is to be forgiving. To be a covering, a balm, a helping hand, a fierce advocate and builder of other women. Being a "sister" means you value other women as you value yourself. That can be problematic if you do not value yourself. But you can learn to love yourself. You can learn to feel worthy and valued. You can learn to trust, love, and support other women even if everything you have experienced in your past or been taught is contrary to that possibility.

Here are five keys to help you *see sisterhood as an action word*:

1. **Cherish the women in your life.** We as women are a gift to each other. Truly a gift. It starts with our mothers, grandmothers, aunts, and other family. Our relationships with other women across the span of our lifetime make us who we are as we become women. Women matter in our lives. They weave together the fabric of our hearts, souls, and minds. They are gifts.

2. **Encourage other women—as well as yourself—to live fully, love passionately, and take risks no matter the price we may pay for happiness.** Life is delicate, precious, and to be lived fully. Better than happiness, we should seek joy.

3. **Celebrate that women are the backbone of life.** There is something amazing about the strength of the "steel" of women. We are the fairer sex, but we are truly the stronger sex. Does anyone want to argue that point?

4. **Thank God for the women in our lives who help us keep it all together.** Women's connection as friends and sisters is powerful. Your true women friends and mentors will love, carry, counsel, and uplift you. And yes, correct you.

5. **Take great pride in helping lift other women as they climb.** Women are graceful, and we are healers. There is no greater love or forgiveness than that of a woman who believes in you and who is in your corner. Successful, loving women possess grace, humility, love, and restoring power. Successful women are not insecure.

Key Words

Sisterhood	Healing	Connection
Grace	Restoration	Friend
Forgiveness	Live	Peace
Lifting	Build	Joy
Encouragement	Give	Power

Section V

The Relational Codes

No Codes determine our ultimate joy, happiness, and fulfillment in life more than the Codes for how we relate to other people. At the end of the day it is our relationships that make our lives worth living.

Code 17

Know Your Front Row

It seems the older we get, the tighter our inner circle becomes. When life has you down, some of those you thought had your back run, others . . . sometimes strangers surprise you and fill that empty space up. Oh, but life has a great balancing act and when that axle turns and you are right side up again . . . you will definitely not be looking for any long, lost "friends" because your inner circle is battle-tested to win!

—Sanjo Jendayi, author, *Girl, Get Empty*

I love this Code. It is one of my paternal grandmother's best lessons to me as a young woman. She told me to build a circle of loyal friends. She told me that friends were the family we choose in life. She taught me to be mindful that not everyone who calls themselves "friend" is one. Your life is like a movie theatre—filled with seats and rows, she said. The people who sit on the front row of your life are the ones who will make or break you. So be careful whom you call friend and where you seat them. Pay attention to who claps when you win. And who does not. Pay attention to those who celebrate you, mourn with you, look after you—and those who do not. Those people need to be moved a few rows back or out the door altogether.

I want you to do something brave. I want you to take a long hard look at the five people closest to you. I'm not talking about your spouse and children, but the five people you talk to the most and spend time with outside of your home. How would you describe them? Are they go-getters? Are they positive? Are they loyal? Are they kind? Do they share your faith? Your values? And your Code? Now take a long hard look at you.

Do they match?

As you look at the people closest to you, I promise you, there will be a mirror. And that mirror will reflect the condition of your own life. If you spend your time around positive, uplifting, and kind people, your life will reflect your own values. Whatever the case, who we surround ourselves with is a reflection of who we are.

Knowing who is in your inner circle—or as the old folks used to say around my Nana's kitchen table, "knowing your row"—is crucial to where you end up in life. Who are the people with whom you surround yourself? Who counsels you matters. It is, in fact, the most crucial aspect to whether or not you will be successful as a friend, as a leader, and as a person. Checking your life row frequently will keep you sharp, powerful, and coachable. Never surround yourself with *yes men* or *yes women*. As the former Mid-Atlantic Regional Director of Alpha Kappa Alpha Sorority, Inc., Dr. Linda H. Gilliam, likes to say, "Yes people will lead you to the water and they will let you drown."

> "Knowing your row" is crucial to where you end up in life.

Show me your front row and I will show you your life. By "row" I mean think of a movie theater and the rows of seats. That is how we often seat people in our lives without even knowing it.

In this Code we will look at what it means to have a "front row" or an inner circle. We'll look at why the people you choose matter so much to who you ultimately become in life. As General Colin Powell wrote so eloquently, "Wise is the person who fortifies his life with the right friendships. If you run with wolves, you will learn how to howl. But, if you associate with eagles, you will learn how to soar to great heights."[1]

We are going to cover three key aspects of knowing who is in your life circle (your front row) and where to place them:

1. How to build a good front row
2. How to spot your frenemies
3. How to remove the wrong people from your front row peacefully

I call my front row my "love counsel," or my "sanctum sanctorum." It is the group I turn to and on whom I rely for advice, wisdom, correction, and encouragement in my life. It is my closest group of confidantes, friends, and supporters. We help each other. We check each other. We develop and sharpen each other. When I look at my five closest associations outside of my mother, I see an amazing group of well-educated, graceful, mature, highly successful women. I see a group of ladies who value loyalty. They value faith. They value family. They value sisterhood. They value honesty. And all of them have overcome adversity. This is my crew. My posse.

> I constantly check my row. Those who don't share my Code get moved back a row each new season until they are moved out of the door. I pay attention to who is with me and who is along for the ride. As should you.

My best friend is a successful small business owner, married over thirty years, and with two grown sons. Another friend foster parents six girls with her husband (a TV personality) while being an author, speaker, radio host, and pastor. The other three are all enormously successful, married, and positive women of faith. Only one of my closest friends is unmarried with no children, like me. We are all upwardly mobile women, shaking up the world, sharing the same Life Code, totally sold out for God, and helping to lift others as we climb. And we have all been friends for ten years or more.

My front row 100 percent reflects my life. The women I run with completely share my Code. They are tested, tried, and true. And my two closest friends are women I aspire to be like with great marriages and families. I adore their husbands, both loyal men of faith with great Codes, who treat me like a beloved younger sister.

I constantly check my row. Those who don't share my Code get moved back a row each new season until they are moved out of the door. I pay attention to who is with me and who is along for the ride. As should you.

How to Build a Good Front Row

You begin building a good front row by being a good person yourself. We really do attract our own kind. Lions roam with lions. Doves fly with doves. Eagles soar with eagles. Like attracts like. If you have a Code, you had better link up with people who share that Code. Your Code is your road map to success.

Stop trying to befriend people or connect with people who do not share your values or your Code.

Look, we all want to know people who expose us to new things, to new experiences, and who create opportunities to grow. BUT, be careful not to get caught up in "similarities." You have to look at people's fruit. What is "fruit," you ask? Your fruit is your character. Your fruit is what you show the world about you. It is also who you are when no one is looking. **Bottom line:** save yourself the heartache of false friends who do not want to do the work of friendship. Friendship also has a Code. It supports, it encourages, it cares, it loves, it protects, it touches, it speaks life, it builds, and it lives.

The way you build a good life row is to be intentional about who you befriend and allow into your most intimate circles. Here are some practical things you should consider when building your "row."

- **Rule 1: You must know someone for at least four seasons before you let them into your networks or space.** Every time I have broken this rule, it has backfired. Our actions must be consistent with our image. It takes time to evaluate this, and it is huge. If, for example, I were the president of a huge multinational corporation, I would be "on" all of the time in the public sphere. I could not go out and get drunk and do things that reflected poorly on me as a leader, or my "brand" (image), or the company I work for and lead. But Code girls understand that our character should never be different in the dark than it is in the light of day. Your character is your Code. They must match 100 percent of the time. If a woman says one thing and lives another, RUN. I am not saying a woman has to be perfect. I sure am not. What I am saying is that women of character are consistent about who they are, what they stand for, and how they live out their Code.

- **Rule 2: You build a great row through your existing networks and connections.** If you are living life by your Code, then you already have at least one amazing person of influence and good character in your life. Build from there. Start connecting with people who are where you want to be in life. But monitor their character. Not all successful women live by a Code of honor and integrity. This kind of woman will never help you. You can be cordial to her, but she should not be in your circle.

- **Rule 3: One of the best indicators you will have of what kind of friend, spouse, business partner, or colleague someone is going to be is to watch how they treat other people.** If they try to resolve conflict through anger and division, you can expect the same when you two have conflict. If a man dislikes or dishonors his mother, you need to pay close attention to that. If people lie, gossip, or trample on others, they will do the same to you. Pay attention to who you allow in your space by how they treat other people in your similar networks or in their own personal and professional lives.

How to Spot Your Frenemies

One of the major ways you can tell that someone in your circle or row is not really for you is by watching how they react to and handle your successes. Your true friends celebrate your success. They send cards, flowers, take you out for dinner, and tell others about you. Your true friends want what is best for you. Your true supporters applaud you when you do well, and they will check you when you are headed down the wrong pathway. Be careful of the "friend" who always has a half smile or a snide comment when you are winning at life.

Case in point: One of my close friends shared a story recently about how her younger sister visited her home and wandered into her private office upstairs, which is full of personal memorabilia, photographs with famous people, awards, and the dozens of framed articles she has published over the years. Her sister, who is not doing so great in her own life, quipped, "I see you have a shrine to yourself." My friend was aghast. She was like, "Huh? You are in my home, looking at my accolades, and you have the nerve to call it a 'shrine'?"

She later confronted her sister and let her know that her comment was not only not appreciated; it was out of order (Code 3: Teach People How to Treat You) and that she has worked very hard for everything in her life. No one has given her anything. She then told her sister to look in the mirror and address her own feelings of unhappiness with her life course.

My friend's story underscores the point that sometimes our own family, spouse, and closest friends can harbor quiet envy toward us. There is a fine line between admiration and envy. And when that envy turns to coveting, ultimately it leads to betrayal and broken connections.

You must be on alert for those people who are in your midst but who are not a part of your mission. They will always be recognizable by what they don't say and what they don't do. Women have to be careful with this because envy and jealousy run high between women. Haters, frenemies— whatever you want to call them—are always looking at what someone else has and feeling bad because they don't have the same thing.

This kind of thinking comes from a place of LACK. If we operate from lack we are looking at what others have that we don't have. When you covet what others have you will always end up hurt, broken, bitter, and envious. You will end up a hater.

> You must be on alert for those people who are in your midst but who are not a part of your mission.

Our true friends know how to celebrate us. They are secure in their own success. That is why it is so crucial to associate with people who are either where you are in life or where you want to be. Successful women (and men) share similar traits:

- They have positivity and a spirit of encouragement.
- They have the ability to elevate others, even above themselves, if needed.
- They are committed to excellence in themselves and in others.
- They don't do petty jealousy or strife.
- They resolve conflict well.

You attract into your life who you are. I took a good look at the front row in my life, and what I realized is that the people I love most, the people who truly have my "back," the people who are there for me through thick and thin are people who share my Code. I have a really good front row. And I have been alert for those who do not mean me well or who simply cannot go where I am headed in life. You must be willing to release people who are not good for you.

How to Remove the Wrong People from Your Front Row Peacefully

If you have someone in your life who can never speak words of encouragement, support you, nurture you, or challenge you to do better, you have the wrong person in your life. Your front row should have people in it who are 100 percent supporters of you. There should never be a doubt about their loyalty, their love, or their longevity.

My advice to you today is to take stock of who is in your front row and who may need to be moved back a few rows, to the rear, or out the door. I assure you that 100 percent of your happiness or unhappiness in life will depend on WHOM you love, WHO loves you, with WHOM you are friends, and WHO is a friend to you. Ask yourself these six questions and make a decision today to only keep those close to you who care for you, lift you, and build you.

1. Is this person there for you when you need her? Are you likewise there for her? You should never have to beg, cajole, or force someone to be kind, to love you, or to care about you.

2. Does this person speak life to you, encourage you, and support your dreams even when you may be in doubt or fear?

3. Can you count on this person to be there in all the seasons of your life, not just the good seasons?

4. Does this person give you lip service? Or heart service? You need people in your life who lead with their hearts.

5. Can you trust this person with your secrets, your reputation, your life, and your heart?

6. Is this person a TRUTH teller? "Wounds from a friend can be trusted, but an enemy multiplies kisses."[2] Never forget that.

Once you have answered these questions you will know who needs to stay and who needs to go. Once you have made the decision to remove someone or place her back a few rows or in the balcony, follow these steps to properly release her.

- Don't make a grand announcement. You don't need to. You simply have to decide if this is someone you *slowly* move back in the rows of your life or if it is someone who is dangerous and needs to be cut off *immediately*. Then act.
- If you decide to untie, let time have its way. Untying means you may want this relationship again if that person changes or grows, or maybe you need a break or a shift in perspective.
- If you decide to cut, do it respectfully. Let them be. Ask them to let you be. Do not gossip. Then be done with it. Learn the lessons this person taught you. And move on.

Deciding to release a relationship is a big deal (see Code 12). So try to do so only after you have cooled off and only after you have given it a great deal of thought and prayer.

Living the Code

What do you do when people in your circle start fighting with each other? This is a common scenario that must be navigated well and carefully. If I am having an "issue" with "A," and it turns ugly, can "B," the mutual friend of us both, love us both and stay loyal to us both without having to choose sides or get stuck in our mess? The answer from my perspective is: *maybe.*

As we get older, the circle of friends and trusted advisers we embrace gets more closed, not more open. This is hard for me, but I am learning it is necessary. I want to end this Code with these questions:

- Can I, or should I, separate myself from people who may not have done anything directly to me but who may have hurt someone in my front row?

- If I have had a bad parting from someone who was once a dear friend or even a not-so-close business associate, do I expect my closest friends and colleagues to now isolate that person as well?

Here are three key things we can strive to do in the above situations to try to maintain our social ties and keep peace with those we love all at once:

1. **Let people prove themselves to you.** Some of the best friends I have ever had came by way of introduction from someone with whom I intentionally no longer associate or keep in touch. Had I cut off certain people because a former friend did not like them or because I had heard "some stuff" about them, I would have blocked some great blessings in my life.

2. **Be a mediator, not a meddler.** Do not pour gasoline on a raging fire. If two friends are at odds, my job as their friend is to HELP them work it through and to heal. Working it through helps all of us to grow. But I must be an objective mediator or I should not mediate at all.

3. **Believe people when they show you who they are.** If you are friends with both Diane and Donna and Diane steals money from Donna, you need to take that as a serious indicator of Diane's bad character on display. Or if Diane gossips about Donna behind her back and smiles in her face, trust that she is doing the same to you.

Our loyalty to our dearest friends, family, and colleagues must be above reproach at all times. But when dealing with "conflict" between friends and colleagues, even family members, we have to be careful not to get drawn into other people's messes. I will take the friend/enemy maxim to heart much more. I will be careful not to unwittingly become an enemy to someone who may turn out down the road to be one of life's best business partners, colleagues, or dearest of friends.

Bottom line: you create a winning life row by operating by a Code of integrity and fair dealing.

Key Words

Life Row	Honor	Listen
Reciprocity	Share	Watch
Code	Together	Encourage
Loyalty	Alike	Motivate
Support	Frenemies	Challenge
Celebration	Haters	Honesty

Code 18

Practice Love, Laughter, Loyalty

When you awaken love and laughter in your life, your mind lets go of fear and anxiety, and your happy spirit becomes the healing balm that transforms every aspect of your human experience.

—Jesse Dylan

Happiness is nothing more than having something to look forward to. Period. Happiness is not a state of being, it is a state of mind. And one of the best medicines any of us can deploy into our lives and into the lives of those we love is to laugh with them, and to be loyal to them. If the challenges of COVID taught us anything in the unforgettable year that was 2020, it should have shown us that life is fragile. Life is short. And that life, most of all, is all about the living of life itself. And as we sheltered in with our families and looked out for our friends and neighbors, we should have learned these truths above all else.

If you live long enough, you begin to understand what's important and what is not.

You understand that at the end of the day everything that matters comes down to people and relationships: the people you love and the people who love you. Our most precious moments come from those we love, those with whom we can laugh, and those who walk with us through the deepest valleys of life. We call those people loyal. We call those people our friends.

Our deep desire, the elusive thing that we chase after most of all, is to be happy. Maybe even deeper than happiness, we seek joy. Although happiness is a choice, joy only comes from deep, abiding, and trusting relationship with your Creator, with others, and with yourself.

> Everything that matters comes down to people and relationships: the people you love and the people who love you.

We are simple creatures. We don't want much, but we crave and value love. We enjoy laughter. We place a premium on loyalty from our men, our families, and even more so from our girlfriends. In this Code, we will look at each of these three *mini Codes* to embrace their value in our lives.

In our Dixie Cup–culture we learn to discard people at the first sign of trouble. This must change if we are to live happy and fulfilled lives. My paternal grandmother was a very wise woman. Although she only had an eighth-grade education, she was an avid reader and very smart. I learned a lot sitting at her knee. Long before inspirational guru Paul McKenna coined "love, loyalty, and laughter" as essential for our happiness, my grandmother taught me about love, she taught me about laughter, and she most certainly taught me about loyalty. These three virtues are at my core. I have learned that leading with love, learning to laugh instead of choosing to lament, and living by an undying Code of loyalty has allowed me to meet people of like mind and spirit who have added immense value to my life.

My "Nana" was the product of the Deep South and of interracial parents at a time when interracial marriage wasn't even lawful in South Carolina. Her parents moved north so they could wed and give her and her older brother a good life. My grandmother later became a single mom, so she understood hard work, sacrifice, and commitment. Her example informed my life at an early age and still does to this day, even though she has now been gone fourteen years.

In this Code we will look at three keys to put the three "L's" into practice in your life. It is one thing to talk about them; it is another thing entirely to live them out day to day. I want to pose three questions that I will answer, but I want you to ponder these questions and come up with your own responses, because these three keys are at the very core of your life. The ability to unlock love, laughter, and loyalty will change your life and take it to heights untold if you will do the work to choose to practice and live in them each day.

1. What's love got to do with it?
2. Why is laughter so good for us?
3. Is loyalty the link that lasts?

What's Love Got to Do with It?

This question made famous by Grammy Award–winning legend Tina Turner from her hit 1993 record by the same name asks the question we have all pondered: What is love anyway, and why do we need it so much? I am no philosopher, but here's my take: Love is that elusive, powerful, intoxicating emotion we crave. Love is who we are. Love is how we were made. Love has everything to do with your journey and mine on this road called life. Love is everything. Everything we want. Everything we need. Everything we desire.

> Love is everything.
> Everything we want.
> Everything we need.
> Everything we desire.

But what does it mean, *to love*? Has it changed? Or is it the same as it always has been? Love in its purest form is an intense feeling of deep affection. But in reality it is something bigger than just a feeling. Love is a verb. It is not passive. Love is an action, it is work, it is commitment, it is unconditional, and it can be hard.

So here is the question we should ask: How can I practice day-to-day love that allows me to get what I need and give it to others? I'll answer the question by sharing what love is to me and what love looks like in my life. Amazing life experiences, loss, and time have taught me that love is everything that is good about us. Love gives us something to look forward to each morning. Love points us to the Creator to look up to and be grateful to each day. And love gives us something to chase after when all is lost. Love is more than a feeling; love is a way of life. And when we practice love in our hearts, with our thoughts, with our words, and most importantly with our actions, we create a groundswell of love from those who surround us. They cannot help it because love is infectious.

My fear, however, is that we have redefined love in a way that is not helpful. Let me explain.

One of the best ways to start is to define what love is *not*. When we are in love, and when we are loved in return, all is right with the world. Nothing can break you when you have love in your life.

> Love is more than a feeling; love is a way of life.

Sadly, we have come to accept imposters masquerading as love. We have replaced love with empty sex. We have replaced love with possessions. We have replaced love with ambition. We have replaced love with self. We have replaced love with busyness. And we have replaced love with idols in our lives. We opt for the easy, the surface, because we know love requires vulnerability. And none of us wants to risk being vulnerable.

Too many of us have forgotten what it means to feel love because we have allowed the pains of our past to stain our hearts. We live carefully and cautiously above the fray. We live close to the outer edge so that no one can really get to know us, and as such never be able to hurt us. The problem with this kind of thinking is it leads to intense loneliness. I know. As I shared in the introduction, I recently had my heart broken when I lost the man I loved.

Love lost can break us. It causes us to draw dangerously inward. It causes us to shut off the possibilities of life. But love is so much more than an emotion. Love is where we live. Make no mistake. It takes courage to love again when you have been hurt. But we must find that courage each and every time, because love is like the air we breathe. It is, as Tony Robbins says, "oxygen to the soul." Love puts the life back in us. Love is the life in us.

So how can we attract the love we want in our lives—not just romantic love but good ole *agape* love; trustworthy sister friend love; healed, whole family love? Here are five steps I am putting into practice in my own life as I dare to find the courage to love again. They are some lessons I'm learning from people I have admired and who live love so well:

1. **You must first *be* love.** You must exude love and offer love to attract love.

2. **You must have healthy boundaries around your heart** (see Code 6). You have to guard your heart, not put a gate on it. When you are emotionally healthy, you attract emotionally healthy people. So if you have a bunch of crazy, damaged, broken people in your life, you need to take a long look at you.

3. **You must love unconditionally.** This one is hard. But it is required. To love unconditionally is not to be a doormat. It is a love that endures in and out of the various seasons of our lives.

4. **You must love hard.** This means you fight for love, you sacrifice for love, and you give in to love. You make yourself vulnerable and allow others to be vulnerable with you.

5. **You must forgive.** Love is forgiveness in motion. It covers. This is the thing about love we struggle with most, but it is the truest form of love when we can forgive and then restore.

At the end of the day (in response to Tina Turner), *love has everything to do with it.* Love has everything to do with us. And love propels us forward. It lives on, and it gives on, long after we are gone.

Why Is Laughter So Good for Us?

As Victor Borge said, "Laughter is the shortest distance between two people." To laugh is to survive. If we can find the laughter in the midst of everything life throws at us, we can survive anything. Laughter sustains our friendships and keeps us tied together. Anyone who knows me well knows I love to laugh and that I can be a bit of an "imp" (my mother's word) to stir up some laughter. I will pull a prank or practical joke in a minute. I can think of nothing I enjoy more than laughter. My hope for every woman reading this book is that she will learn to laugh. Truly laugh from her core, from her deepest place, and make it part of her Life Code.

Laughter has practical life and health benefits, just like her first cousin, love. When we are full of laughter we are actually laughing inside. You know the kind of laugh that makes you fall on the floor or spit your coffee across the room. When laughter is shared, it binds people together and increases happiness and intimacy. Laughter triggers healthy physical changes in the body. Humor and laughter, according to medical researchers, strengthen your immune system, boost your energy, diminish pain, and protect you from the damaging effects of stress. Best of all, a cheerful heart, as the Proverbs writer wrote long ago, is "good medicine."[1] Or as William James once penned, "We don't laugh because we're happy; we're happy because we laugh."[2]

Laughter is a powerful antidote to stress, pain, and conflict. Nothing works faster or more dependably to bring your mind and body back into balance than a good laugh. Humor lightens your burdens, inspires hope, connects you to others, and keeps you grounded, focused, and alert.

Here are some practical effects of laughter in your life:

- Laughter relaxes the body. A good laugh relieves physical tension and stress, leaving your muscles relaxed for up to forty-five minutes afterward.

- Laughter strengthens the immune system. It reduces stress hormones and increases immune cells and infection-fighting antibodies, improving your resistance to disease.

- Laughter triggers the release of endorphins, which promote an overall sense of well-being and can even temporarily relieve pain.

- Laughter protects the heart. It improves the function of blood vessels and increases blood flow, which can help protect against a heart attack and other cardiovascular problems.[3]

Laughter is usually spontaneous. But there are ways you can make laughter a part of your life. There are things we can do to make sure that, just as we take our vitamins each day or head to the gym, we intentionally expose ourselves to laughter.

Here are five keys I learned from one of my mentors for how to put a daily spark of laughter in my life:

1. Every week she watches a favorite romantic comedy that makes her laugh out loud.
2. She takes a walk on her lunch break to a nearby day care playground and watches little kids play.
3. She and her husband spend intentional play time with their dogs daily (their kids are grown).
4. She and her girlfriends go once a month to a karaoke night (none of them sings well).
5. She surrounds herself with people who have a great sense of humor, laughter, and levity in their lives.

These tips are a great starting point, but whatever makes you smile, makes you chuckle, or makes you giggle should be developed as a daily or weekly routine in your life. Laughter really does make us lighter. It lifts us and connects us to other people.

Is Loyalty the Link That Lasts?

Loyalty is the distant relative of love and laughter. Loyalty has the hard job. Love and laughter are the best of us. And they bring out the best in us. But *loyalty* is a word we don't use much anymore in our disposable culture. Like many ancient Codes, loyalty has taken a back seat to "PC" (political correctness), expediency, and self-advancement. But loyalty is where the rubber meets the road. Loyalty is unconditional love put into practice. Loyalty is what happens when we would rather take the easy road or the popular path but instead find ourselves following the righteous cause, the passionate leader, or the person we love.

> There is nothing more valuable, more rewarding, and more needed today than loyalty. It is more valuable than money or power. You cannot buy loyalty because loyalty is never for sale.

Loyalty is for me, *reflex*. It is part of my Code. Loyalty isn't easy. It will cost you something. But if you are loyal to the right people (Code 17, Know Your Front Row) you will receive loyalty in return. And there is nothing more valuable, more rewarding, and more needed today than loyalty. It is more valuable than money or power. You cannot buy loyalty because loyalty is never for sale.

Loyalty is the state of being faithful, devoted, or committed to something or someone. It means having *allegiance* to something bigger than ourselves, like our country or a cause. Loyalty, like love and laughter, must be nurtured and practiced daily. Loyalty is never fleeting, negotiable, or unwise. Loyalty endures. It corrects. And it protects.

In a survey of both men and woman, according to the AskMen. com Great Male Survey, 2009 Edition, and Yahoo! Shine Great Female Survey, 2009 Edition, a sense of loyalty is the most important personality trait making a man or woman "relationship material." For men, a sense of loyalty (32%) outranked a sense of caring/

nurturing (24%), a sense of humor (23%), and intelligence (21%). For women, a sense of loyalty (34%) outranked a sense of nurturing/caring (31%), a sense of humor (22%), intelligence (10%), and other (3%).[4] This survey shows us that men and women share the same Code when it comes to the value of loyalty.

Loyalty requires discernment. As Dr. Brené Brown says:

> Our stories are not meant for everyone. Hearing them is a privilege, and we should always ask ourselves this before we share: "Who has earned the right to hear my story?" If we have one or two people in our lives who can sit with us and hold space for our shame stories, and love us for our strengths and struggles, we are incredibly lucky. If we have a friend, or small group of friends, or family who embraces our imperfections, vulnerabilities, and power, and fills us with a sense of belonging, we are incredibly lucky.[5]

Make sure that you are giving your loyalty and sharing your life stories with people deserving of the gift of you. The ten traits of a loyal woman are as follows:

1. She is loyal first to herself, to her dream, and to her desires. This is key because it allows her to want those same things for the people in her life and be willing to help them get there.
2. She honors her word and her commitments.
3. She is trustworthy.
4. She is honest.
5. She is consistent and reliable.
6. She defends those she works for, is in partnership with, or in relationship with.
7. She corrects or challenges those she loves in private but defends them fiercely in public.
8. She is there in the valleys, walking by her friends' side, and is there on the mountaintop, pulling them up and applauding their arrival.

9. She is a woman of honor. She does not do "lukewarm." She takes sides when it is right to do so. She will never leave her friends or family on the battlefield alone.

10. She has a Code. And it is fierce. It does not depend on what is in it for her. Her Code is what her friends and family love about her. It is what makes her loyal.

Living the Code

Love, laughter, and loyalty. Who can live without them? Who would want to? They are the wellspring of our lives. I encourage you to work at these three. See them as daily vitamins that strengthen the core of your life.

Love: The most important thing about love is to *be present*. Our lives are short. We miss a lot as busy, overwhelmed women. Slow down. Smell the roses. We all want to give and receive love. I believe the biggest barrier to us not getting the love we desire is the unhealed pains of our past (see Code 2). We must intentionally tear down the barriers to love in our lives. Anything that comes between you and love must be removed quickly from your life.

Laughter: Sharing laughter is one of the most effective keys for unlocking excitement and joy in our relationships. Sharing laughter adds life-sustaining vitality and resilience to our lives. Laughter is also a powerful and effective way to heal resentments, disagreements, and hurts.

- Laughter eliminates toxic emotions. You can't feel anxious, angry, or sad when you're laughing.

- Laughter helps you to rejuvenate. It reduces stress and increases energy, enabling you to stay focused and accomplish more.

- Laughter shifts your view, allowing you to see situations in a more realistic, less threatening light. A humorous perspective creates psychological distance, which can help you avoid feeling overwhelmed.

Loyalty: The ability to remain loyal is one of life's most precious Codes. It is a learned behavior, however, that comes from feeling connected, engaged, and loved by others. Loyalty is all about your Code. Loyalty looks and acts a certain way. I'll say this again: *you cannot buy loyalty because loyalty is never for sale.*

🔑 Key Words

Love	Humor	Barriers
Laughter	Joy	Committed
Loyalty	Connection	Faithful
Faithfulness	Defenses	Healing

Code
19

Have Courageous
Conversations

Difficult conversations are almost never about getting the facts right.
They are about conflicting perceptions, interpretations, and values.

People almost never change without first feeling understood.

—Douglas Stone, author, *Difficult Conversations:
How to Discuss What Matters Most*

I used to struggle with speaking my mind, or my heart for that matter. I no longer do so. Gratefully, as we age and mature we learn the value of being authentic with ourselves most of all. We learn the life-changing power of saying what we need to say, of listening, of growing, and of wanting to work things through with those we love. We learn that to suppress emotions is to suffocate the soul. That to not say the words out loud is to betray yourself. In my family, we were taught to ignore, deny, and cover. Three of the most dangerous ways not to communicate your feelings and to guarantee that you will struggle in all of your interpersonal relationships throughout the course of your life, if you do not course correct early on.

There is a big difference between communication and conversation.

We need to learn this distinction well.

We spend too much of our time now over communicating with the gadgets at our fingertips. But the real question is, have we stopped talking to one another in ways that truly matter?

I think so.

The truth is, we are all weary travelers on this new communication highway. Maybe not the very young among us who have no frame of reference for what it was like when conversation was all we had. But those of us old enough to remember what it was like to talk all night on the phone or to be courted by a young man who came to our house, met our parents, and promised to have us home by 11:00 p.m. feel the absence of good old-fashioned, face-to-face, heart-to-heart, connected conversation. And make no mistake, there are serious side effects from this lack of talking.

The most obvious and dangerous side effect is the fact that we are much too quick to "cut off" people in a moment's anger or offense. We don't pick up the phone and talk. How ironic that we yearn for meaningful, honest, and compelling conversation, yet fail to act on it when it is most needed. We yearn for the connection that can only come when two souls agree and dare to express themselves freely. Yet, we run and hide. And we ruin ourselves because we refuse to talk.

For some unknown reason we do the opposite of what we want to do. We let the voice of fear tell us that we will be rejected or ignored, that an argument will ensue, or that the other person won't care how we feel. So we get them before they get us. We revert to acting like children playing in a sandbox instead of learning how to step back, gain perspective, and get more information before we throw away someone who matters. How ironic that we would rather lose someone of value than to admit we were wrong, apologize (see Code 10), and seek reconciliation. For some reason, we have stopped asking the hard questions. We simply do not want to "talk" anymore.

The fact of the matter is this: *you will never be able to have a successful relationship of any kind without equally successful authentic and open conversation.*

Tragically, we've replaced conversation with excessive, abrupt, often-abrasive communication via text, email, or social media. When I was a young woman in my twenties, you couldn't break up with a guy (or be broken up with) by text, and you couldn't send your best friend an angry email or post your emotions on Facebook or Twitter. The only way you could communicate your feelings was to have a conversation on the telephone, in person, or by letter.

> We've replaced conversation with excessive, abrupt, often-abrasive communication via text, email, or social media.

Fast-forward to our gadget-laden world. We all know that on some deep level we have lost our ability to engage in meaningful, respectful, and powerful dialogue with other people. We all know how to communicate (or so we think) with our gadgets, but we have lost the art of private, peaceful, and passionate conversation in our marriages, with our friends, in our families, in the church, and in our careers. Truth be told, ladies, we have become a sisterhood of cowards when it comes to one-on-one conversations and what I call "courageous conversations."

A crucial part of being successful in the art of "conversation" is to be willing to be vulnerable, open, and transparent, and most importantly, allow others to do the same. In this Code we will look at two keys you need to have meaningful, transformative, and honest conversations:

1. How communication and conversation differ
2. What courageous conversations are

How Communication and Conversation Differ

Communication is conveying information through the exchange of thoughts or messages, or by speech, visuals, signals, writing, or behavior. Conversation, however, is defined as *talking to* another person through an informal or formal exchange of thoughts through *spoken words.*[1] The key difference between communication and conversation is that one actually includes "talking." This is an important distinction we have forgotten. Yes, texting is communicating. Yes, Facebook posts and tweets communicate how we think or feel. But nothing—and I mean nothing—replaces the timeless Code of talking to another person, one-on-one, or even through a mediator, if needed. Nothing replaces the connection of conversation.

Pause here and reflect. When was the last time you talked to someone about what you needed? About how you felt? About your dreams, your hopes, your fears? When was the last time you let someone inside your soul's landscape to see the real you? If it has been a while, I want to encourage you (and myself) to consider this: Life is short. Very. Even if you live to be 100, that is nothing compared to eternity.

So what are we waiting for?

Say what you need to say. Speak up. You have nothing to lose and everything to gain by sharing what you think, what you want, and what you need. And by doing so, you will encourage others to share the same with you about themselves. Sisters of the Code, it is time for us to get beyond the surface, the senseless chatter of communication, and delve into the deep waters of conversation once again.

Here's a quick story about a former colleague of mine who had a penchant for sending "reply to all" emails at work.

This woman is brilliant, talented, and hardworking. But at the time I knew her, she did not know how to win friends and influence people. One day Melody had had her fill of the mishaps of her subordinates. Always pretty hard-nosed, Melody was known for stinging emails. This day she decided to obliterate a female colleague, who was her junior, via email, and do it "in front of" the firm's biggest partners. Even though much of what she wrote was true, the way she decided to communicate boomeranged on Melody, and she was quietly fired within weeks.

Here's the point: there was a better way for Melody to communicate. First, she was out of order to humiliate another woman in front of her colleagues and superiors. Second, she did not seek to help the young woman to do better; instead, she opted to broadcast her emotions for all to see. A better pathway for Melody would have been to have a conversation with her team, with the person in question, and with the partners offline. The fact that she did not do so cost her reputation, her job, and her own pathway to partnership. The lesson for all of us in this, particularly as women, is that we cannot allow our need to communicate to override the importance of what is best said when we converse.

What Courageous Conversations Are

A courageous conversation is one that we would rather avoid because we know it may cost us something or someone if we dare to say what needs to be said or to hear what needs to be heard. What it is not is someone dumping on you, ranting on you, going off on you, or tearing you down.

As *Fix My Life* guru Iyanla Vanzant likes to say, "It is NOT a 'hard conversation' unless the relationship matters." I agree. It's easy to talk or not talk to someone in whom we have no emotional investment or connection. Hard conversations occur in important relationships where information needs to be shared, clarity gained, or feelings expressed. And let me be clear, it is wrong, inappropriate, and downright unsisterly to send someone an email, text, or other form of communication when a conversation is required. It is also very wrong to talk to others about the person you need to talk to. This gets into Code 9: Do Not Gossip.

According to coaching expert Laurie Gerber, we need to stop having one-sided conversations in our heads.

> Most people convince themselves that it's safer to avoid hard con-versations, ignore the issue and try to forget about it. The prob-lem is that we are human, and most of us don't forget. Instead, we harbor bad feelings and then feel the need to validate them. Conflicts and complaints escalate in the silence. By playing both sides of the dialogue in your head, you turn the other person into a pawn. They have no voice, no feelings and no ability to state their opinion. You are only focused on a perceived injustice to you and forget about the importance of the relationship. This scenario does nothing productive, but it gives you all the power—which is why you do it![2]

So let's get into WHY we need to have courageous conversations, and then in the Living the Code section we will address HOW to have them. First, let's adopt a rule: having a much-needed conversa-tion is crucial no matter what the outcome. Cowards say I CAN'T talk it out. Women of courage say I MUST talk it out in order to honor myself and my Code. If, however, the other person does not wish to engage in such a dialogue, then we have to accept that and do our best to move on. Sometimes, Sisters, we are not going to get closure. Sometimes we will not get to have that conversation we so desperately desire.

Here are two rules of thumb you should use in deciding whether a courageous conversation is called for:

1. If a relationship or person you value is in jeopardy due to poor communication and the lack of authentic conversation, you should fight to keep it healthy. Find the courage to talk.

2. If, on the other hand, a relationship or professional alliance has run its course, it is the responsible thing to bring closure

to a challenging conflict with someone you once loved or valued. Find a way to tell them why you are ending the relationship, and do so with grace, class, and empathy. This is critical because this gets to what we discussed in Codes 12 (Never Cut What You Can Untie) and 17 (Know Your Front Row): it matters how we exit our relationships.

The Golden Rule—treat others how you want to be treated—still stands. Have you ever been dropped? Discarded without a word? Cut off by someone you trusted, loved, or thought was a dear friend? How does it feel? It feels horrible, right?

Don't do that to others. Talking things out allows you both to grow. It challenges you, but it strengthens your interpersonal skills. It transforms. It heals, and it can lead to amazing restoration and stronger ties once everything that needs to be said is said and received with an open heart. Talking it out with courage, respect, and love may not mean you can mend things, but it allows you to move forward whole.

Mali is from Thailand. She and her husband, Aran, own a successful chain of hair spas. Mali is in her midfifties and was raised in a culture where women did not make demands on their men and took care of everyone but themselves. Mali and Aran had an unhappy marriage for years. Aran had a secret porn addiction that was not so secret to his wife. Yet they were both loving parents to their three teenage sons. Aran could be abrasive to Mali, unloving, and downright mean even in front of their customers. Mali told a group of her friends that she had had enough and wanted to leave, but she was afraid of what her family would say and how it would impact their business. Her best friend, Sue, encouraged Mali to have the "hard conversation" with Aran before she just left her marriage of twenty-five years.

Mali took the advice, got a marriage counselor at their church, and set a date for a couple's intervention. Aran was not happy at first, but the counselor made it clear to him that if he did not start listening to and communicating with his wife through intimate conversations, their marriage was at a dead end. Aran agreed to the counseling.

Mali opened up and he listened. Aran opened up and she listened. What they discovered was that they had both been badly hurt as children (both sexually and emotionally abused) and that they had both been taught to cover their feelings. By going to counseling and having a "hard conversation," Mali and Aran grew closer. Their prayer life got stronger. They resumed a healthy sex life. They learned to laugh, share, and really talk to one another. To see them now is to smile. Their marriage was saved through the art of courageous conversation with the help of a trained professional.

Here is the point: it has become quite common to see couples divorce, friendships break apart, business relationships turn sour, and even siblings stop speaking to one another for years over the smallest things. We don't want to do the necessary work—and yes, the hard work—of wrestling through our "issues," extending grace, asking for forgiveness, learning how to apologize effectively, being humble, and understanding that people are flawed (as are we). And that you can't just love people when they are good; you have to love them when they make mistakes. If we don't get this right and rediscover what it means to talk it out before we walk out, we are going to be a species of broken, angry, bitter, and lonely people.

The problem with this kind of thinking is that it leaves us broken, unhealed, and empty. We may think it is better to walk away than to deal with what is wrong in our relationships, but it is not. Psychologists and medical doctors will tell you that not talking out your problems and not learning to manage your human relationships well will only result in broken hearts, resentment, and anger, which lead directly to physical illness, emotional stress, and sometimes worse. For me, though, it's much simpler than that. I have found that when I don't take the time to have that "courageous conversation" or have that long overdue talk, I am the one who loses in the long run, not the person I cast out.

Here's the thing: the only way we grow into better human beings is by facing ourselves and facing our problems so that we can fix them. Talking is one of the most soul-lifting, healing, and connecting things we can do. Talking it out before you walk out allows you to see, feel, and touch another's soul landscape. Even if you two or three ultimately decide that the relationship cannot be saved, at least you know that you had the conversation. You communicated. You cared enough to hear someone out and to be heard out by them. It matters how we exit our relationships. If we get into unhealthy patterns of throwing people away, or cutting them off without so much as a word, we damage ourselves and we damage other people.

> The only way we grow into better human beings is by facing ourselves and facing our problems so that we can fix them. Talking is one of the most soul-lifting, healing, and connecting things we can do.

Our goal has to be to find the courage *every day* to say what needs to be said. We need to practice being a person who has hard, courageous conversations. Most people wait until they're on their deathbed or when the situation becomes acute to have a difficult conversation. That is not a good way to live. We need to have conversations whenever the need arises. Practicing conversation is a great way to kill remorse, and to keep regret or resentments from festering. Being honest isn't always easy, but people will respect you as someone who faces issues and situations head-on. The right people will admire and emulate your model.

If you are having a one-sided conversation in your head right now about someone or something, don't. If at all possible, go to the person and have a real conversation about the issue. It will heal your heart.

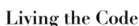

Living the Code

Now that we know what a conversation entails, are we ready to have one? I watch trends on social media and the BIGGEST trend I see is people who have been broken and angered by relationships that have gone bad playing it out on social media or via texts. It leaves people wounded deeply because someone thought they weren't worthy of a conversation.

In addition, conversation is good for your health. Talking and sharing is one of the most healthy, natural, spiritual endeavors we can undertake. It connects us to that other person. Face-to-face conversations are the most desirable because you can read body language, see their eyes, understand their heart, and vice versa.

Here are some keys you can begin to implement as you communicate with others. I try to live by these simple rules when it comes to talking things out before I walk out.

1. **Cool off. Gain perspective.** Take a minute, pray, seek wise and experienced counsel, and then approach the person to have a face-to-face conversation, a Skype call, or at least a phone call. Do not resolve your conflicts or concerns by text or email.

2. **Let love and empathy set the tone.** If you love someone, you have to let those be the first words you utter when you are preparing to address your "issues." You also have to shift from a place of "I don't understand" to "Help me understand." Affirm people you love. Do not attack them. Insist on the same respect for yourself. People will listen to us when we speak to them from a place of compassion and grace versus one of condemnation and judgment.

3. **Get help from a trusted mediator or friend.** If you two cannot talk it out alone, look to trusted friends, clergy, or counselors who have BOTH of your best interests in mind and who want to see you both heal and move forward. Do not allow gossips

or biased parties to "mediate." They will only deepen the damage.

4. **Write a letter if conversation fails.** Finally, writing a letter can be a great way to let someone know how you feel. But write a few drafts, run it by a trusted friend, pray on it, sleep on it, then mail it. And allow that person to write back to you. Hopefully what results is a conversation, a connection, and a healing no matter what you decide to do with the relationship. It is important to release people the right way.

Bottom line: talk before you walk. People who can walk away from you are simply not for you. Those who love us and those we love are worth the fight. They are worth the work. They are worth the understanding and listening of our hearts. Conversation is how we connect as human beings.

Finally here are five practical steps I've used with both corporate and individual clients to facilitate courageous conversations:

1. **Ask for permission and set a time to talk.** When you are ready to have a hard conversation with a person, it's important to ask for their buy-in, and without it there can be no conversation. Timing is key. And it has to be right for both parties.

2. **Establish ground rules.** You must approach a difficult conversation with a goal in mind. No matter the outcome, they must know your intention is positive and honoring of your history.

3. **Stay open to what you don't know.** When people get stuck or offended it's usually because they lack proper context and information. Stay open to what you may not know that can shed light on what causes the challenge in the relationship.

4. **Say what you need to say.** Time is short. Regrets lead to stress, brokenness, and bitterness. John Mayer's song, "Say," says it all. Say what needs to be said, and let them have their say too.

5. **Find restoration and release.** The amazing thing about courageous conversations is that they either free us to release the

relationship or they help us to grow deeper in our intimacy and relationships.

🔑 Key Words

Communication	Growth	Listening
Conversation	Exchange	Sharing
Intimacy	Verbal	Hearing
Vulnerability	Talking	Courage

Reconnect with Your Life

Go for a walk outdoors. Reconnect with the feeling of the wind blowing through your hair. Listen to the birds that live in a tree in your yard. Watch the sunset. Take time to smell the flowers that bloom in the park during the summer. The natural world is just as natural as it ever was, except there is less of it than there was twenty-five years ago—and most of us don't make a point of enjoying it often enough.

—Skye Alexander

I would like to think that COVID was a game changer for all of us as human beings, all over this globe. But most of all, for us as women. Labor and economic data shows that women were the hardest hit by the pandemic professionally, personally, and emotionally as caregivers, mothers, and providers. And we paid and are still paying a terrible emotional price. I can speak for myself: I had a sick parent at home for a year; I had to keep my business running; I lost significant income. And yet, despite it all, I rediscovered me. I rediscovered nature. Quiet. Connection with friends and family. I slowed down. I could hear my heart beat again. Being stuck inside forced us all to reflect on self. To take care of self. To realize that if I do not reconnect with me and what I need and what I desire, I will be no good for anyone else.

Every woman wants to be loved and to love. To be valued and to value others. And to find purpose and meaning in her living. All of these desires can only be realized when we are connected first to ourselves and second to others.

The goal of your life should be the search for your life. It is to be present in the moments of life instead of being consumed by the big, loud distractions of life. When you connect with yourself, you are taking a leap into your soul landscape, and you are exploring your human spirit—your dreams and your desires. Connection, then, is our most basic need right after love. Our desire for connection is a deep hunger that is never quite satisfied. It lasts throughout our lifetime, and if we miss love and connection with other people, some say we miss life itself. Our longing for other people sets us apart from all other species and without connection we wither and we die, literally, figuratively, or both.

Yet something has gone wrong.

Women are torn because we've been offered a *false choice* between having "status," "success," and "stuff" versus having to *give it all up* so that we can spend more quality time with ourselves, our families, and our friends. This choice is not based in reality. It is based in an image of what women should be.

But here is the truth: you don't have to choose the pursuit of "success" over sacred time with yourself or with your family. One of the definitions of success must be that we have the power to choose how we invest not just in our work but in ourselves. We can no longer relegate our needs or our loved ones to second-class status. In short, *to reconnect is to rediscover the life in living.*

Our success has come with a price. We travel the world, run businesses, pursue our dreams, and live out our life's purpose in ways our mothers never imagined, but there is still an expectation that we will be nurturing and always available to those who need us. We know that it is not always easy to be so readily available. And we hate ourselves for it. We feel guilty. We feel less than. We feel shortchanged on the one hand and rich on the other.

It is time to put the guilt aside. It is time to take care of you. But you cannot effectively *nurture yourself* when you won't slow down long enough to *know yourself*. Don't miss that one, Sisters. It's huge. In this chapter, we will look at how to integrate our lives as friends, wives, mothers, sisters, and daughters without neglecting ourselves. I believe that it is through our "connections" with those we love and value that we build our lives in ways that lead us to the greatest success and satisfaction. Without people to share our lives, success, status, and stuff mean nothing.

Gone are the days when women could focus on one thing at a time—namely, our families. Today's woman is all about the process of making all the parts of her life work together well. Every day we look at our to-do list and we decide who and what comes first. We recognize as part of our daily routine that nurturing our relationships is a life enhancer, not a time stealer. We know that relationships enhance our lives, and we are nothing without the people we love.

Code 1 makes it clear that we are nothing if we do not first value ourselves. You must make time for you a priority. You have to restore your spirit, release stress, and take care of your mind, body, and soul because no one else will. We begin to see our interactions with other people as the fuel we need to keep going. If you are in unhealthy relationships, you must commit to release them. Gently and respectfully, but release them you must.

Women have arrived. We are shattering glass ceilings, tearing down brick walls, and jumping over barbed wire fences all around the world. Yet somewhere deep in our spirit, we worry that we are missing something. We worry that we are neglecting the most basic Code: the desire to love and to be loved; the desire to take care of and nurture our families; and the desire to cultivate meaningful friendships and connections that will last a lifetime.

Women value connection. We value friendship. We value family. Yet we also want to be winners. We want to work and succeed at all we do. Try as we might, we simply cannot, as the old commercial said, bring home the bacon, fry it up in the pan, and never let him forget he's a man! Hence, we think we are forced to choose one or the other. Our male counterparts never feel the need to choose.

We no longer have to choose. It's always been a false choice. When we live by a Code, we are clear. Our relationships are sacrosanct.

As we approach how we reconnect, let's keep these keys in mind:

1. Making time for yourself, your family, and your friends is a priority.
2. Building healthy relationships enhances your health, your career, and your spirit.

Making Time for Yourself, Your Family, and Your Friends Is a Priority

People are on edge. They feel disconnected and they are angry about it. You see it everywhere—people leveling attacks on Facebook and Twitter, unfriending and unfollowing and deleting people or blocking them. We live in a culture that celebrates "cutting people off" instantaneously.

One of our favorite expressions of the twenty-first century is "It is what it is." I use this saying far too often and I catch myself. It is our way of saying I am powerless, I refuse to engage, and I cannot change it, so why bother? Truly, we have become like weary soldiers on the battlefield of life who have surrendered to an acceptance of living life for what "it is" versus what we all desperately want and need it "to be."

Stop for a moment and look around you. Go into a restaurant or doctor's waiting room and you will see people glued to electronic gadgets, all designed supposedly to "connect us," while we ignore the flesh-and-blood people sitting right across from us.

Now go watch the kids playing on the playground. Something magical is taking place—these toddlers are holding hands, wrestling with each other, touching, sharing food and juice boxes. They are laughing, singing, and engaging one another fully. This is who we should be at our core. These tiny humans grow up to be us, when we should be more like they are. The goal of this Code is to explore why being isolated and disconnected has become so common, why it's so damaging to us and our relationships, and how we can get back to the childlike innocence of love and human connection.

We all feel disconnected on some level from our kids, our parents, our colleagues, our spouses or boyfriends, our life's purpose, and our authentic selves. We want to return to a simpler time when people talked about their day, spent quality time together, and relaxed. We are tired of hiding behind our gadgets. We are tired of being exhausted and isolated. We hate that every communication we get now comes as a text, email, or instant message. We long to reconnect.

Every once in a while, we find glimpses of shared humanity. When we hear about a tragic national event or experience the sudden loss of a loved one, a colleague, a job, our home, or our health, the light bulb goes on. We resolve that we will do better. We grab our loved ones and we hold on ever so tight. But in a few weeks we go right back to being disconnected. The truth is, we don't like to face our humanity or our mortality because it means we will have to slow down and be accountable for the choices we make.

> Every once in a while, we find glimpses of shared humanity.

And who has time for that? We are too distracted and too busy to connect with other people. And we wonder why depression is an epidemic of sorts in this country and why one in five people is on antidepressants, divorce is rampant, abuse is widespread in our relationships, workplace violence is on the rise, and on and on. We who live in the most advanced age the world has ever seen have a very serious problem connecting one-on-one with other people.

That is the disconnected mind-set that needs to change or it will destroy us. We reconnect to others by making a decision. There is power in making a decision. It allows us to get free from what we fear we do not have enough time to do, and it empowers us to act on what we truly want to do. Change starts with the intention to be present and to reconnect with what defines our lives as human beings.

This is where understanding what the Code is all about comes in. The women of our mothers' and grandmothers' days understood their Code, for their time:

- My family comes first.
- My friends come second.
- My self comes last.

While many of us still hold to this basic Code, we do so begrudgingly. And rightly so; self should never come last. In the safety announcements on a plane, the flight attendant tells you to put your own oxygen mask on first. If you do not take care of your needs first, you will be of little value to everyone else.

We do not intentionally take people for granted or neglect those closest to us. It is just the nature of the beast. We have replaced talking with texting and handwritten notes with e-cards. We have replaced quality time with "social networking." Our mothers and grandmothers probably resented having to put their dreams and desires last. They whisper to us that they admire our freedom; they admire our success, our status, and even our "stuff." What they *do not* admire is our weariness, our disconnectedness, our stress, and our strain. They do not admire how we try to be all things to all people and end up being of little good to anyone.

Their generations valued friendships. They valued sharing a cup of coffee and talking for hours. They did not text; they talked. They nurtured all of their relationships as building blocks for their lives. People mattered more than power or pursuits. Family, both immediate and extended, was cared for and supported no matter what. Grandparents, aunts, and uncles came to live with them as they aged or became infirm. It was their Code, and they lived it faithfully and without complaint.

Hence, they see us as a confused and restless lot. We are confused about what we should value when it comes to our desire to be out and about in the world, juxtaposed against our understanding that life is short, time is precious, and our families and friends should be our primary focus in life. Unfortunately, this confusion starts from a contrived concept about what it means to be a modern woman. Instead of embracing this contrived concept, we should be embracing our Code.

The truth is, *we can't have it all* as women—or as men, for that matter. Most importantly, maybe we should not want to have it all. In the pursuit to be better, or best, something and someone will always get left behind or left out. Once we accept that truth, we can begin to make decisions about what we value and in what order we put those values.

Building Healthy Relationships Enhances Your Health, Your Career, and Your Spirit

Two Women; Two Outcomes

Cynthia is a thirty-seven-year-old mother of twin teenage boys. She runs a successful stationery store in a quaint village in Virginia. Her husband, who is in his forties, is a major executive at a

Fortune 100 company, and he travels the world at least half of the year. Cynthia works at the store night and day, and when she is home she is always working on marketing campaigns, new lines of stationery, and how she can grow the business online.

Two years ago, Cynthia's mom had a massive stroke. She spent months in rehab and had to move in with her daughter and son-in law. Cynthia's marriage started to experience strain due to the long hours and travel both she and her husband put in. Her boys were thriving in school and in sports, but they were disconnected from their parents, who were never "there," even when they were around. Suddenly, Cynthia's world started to fall apart.

This past summer, I went into the stationery store and saw a "going out of business" sign. I asked, "Why are you closing the shop?" She said, "Sophia, I had an *aha* moment. I am missing life. I am missing what and who matters in my life. Time is short. I have a rare opportunity to travel the world with the man I love and I've been given the gift of more years with Mom. Later I may start a new business, but only after I reconnect with my family and my friends."

Diane, on the other hand, knew what she wanted. She is the envy of her friends, family, and church circle. She is an attorney at a large law firm. Yet, from the moment she graduated law school, Diane had a plan. She wanted to be married, have kids, and be close to her aging parents. She was intentional about "life integration." She was intentional about family time, faith time, girl time, and career building. Diane put in the long hours expected of her as an associate, but when she was off work, she was off work. She integrated her life well by carving out time for the people who mattered. She looked forward to her time with her loved ones. She viewed them as a respite in life's storms. She viewed their time together as refueling for her soul. And she guarded that time fiercely, just as she did not allow her personal commitments to intrude on her work obligations.

Diane is now forty and she has two small children. Her marriage is strong. Her husband helps with the kids. She is married to a man who also believes in work-life integration. They are committed to the notion that says family and friends are a crucial part of our lives. Diane has built her life on the Code that says she did not have to choose one or the other, career versus family or family at the expense of a thriving law career. Diane gets tired too. And yes, she is busy. But she has made a decision to make her life work the way she wants by integrating all the parts of her life into a daily life routine.

The Power of Reconnection

We are built for love, for connection, for relationship, and for fellowship with other people. Of all the Codes in this book, Code 20 is the epicenter of where we live. We connect most deeply with other people when we can be vulnerable, when we can be open, and when we can truly share ourselves—in some ways bare ourselves to other people.

Think about the times in your life that hold the most meaning for you. Your fondest memories, achievements, and triumphs involve being with the people you love. Ladies, it's time to "integrate" our living, loving, and laughing with ourselves and with the people we meet along the journey called life. It's time to make relationships a priority again. It's time to reconnect.

I know life can be hard. The connections in my life, the amazing women in my life, have propelled me to every success, through every comeback and every new beginning. We women need each other now more than ever. We need sister circles. We need friendships. We need support. We need coaching. We need information. We need connected, courageous conversations. We need meaningful touch. We need rest. We need our families, and we need our friends.

Single moms, I know you are doing your best. I know that we all wish we had more time with those we love. We may love to stay home if we could, raise our kids, not miss any of their precious moments. We are busy. We are making things happen. We are changing the world. But we have to ask ourselves, and without guilt and condemnation, *Can I afford NOT to spend more time with my kids, my loved ones, and my closest friends?*

I think we can all agree the answer to that question is no. Today, start making a life integration plan wherever you are. As the old Nike "Just Do It" ad that I carry in my wallet to this day says, "It's never too late to have a life. And never too late to change one."

Living the Code

Here are some key takeaways from Code 20: Reconnect with Your Life. Use these key action steps to help you put these strategies into practice. These are five of my favorites that I am implementing daily into my own life:

1. **Intentionally connect with family and friends.** Our lives are not just about achieving success, accumulating stuff, or our career. Life is also about connecting on a more intimate and spiritual level with family and friends. It starts by being intentional. The idea of "work-life balance" is a myth. Life is not about balance as much as it is about making it all work at the same time by seeing the various pieces of our lives as puzzle pieces that fit neatly together to build the picture of our lives.

2. **Stop running and doing and start taking care of yourself.** You and I can only give our best to our valued relationships when we are rested, restored, and rejuvenated. Code 20 is directly

linked to Codes 1, 4, and 5. You will not have meaningful relationships until you take care of yourself.

3. **Take the time to connect with people.** Building relationships takes work and it takes time. Talk to people; engage them. When we allow others to invest in us, it will inspire us to build a better home. A better purpose. A better family. A better career. A better friend network and a better social circle. We need one another. We are hardwired for social connection. We are not meant to live life alone. And be willing to learn from them. It will transform your life.

4. **Build meaningful relationships with yourself and with others.** Make this a matter of priority. It is a healthy choice for us. Science has proven time and time again that we live longer and healthier when we are happy, connected, and in good, solid relationships.

5. **Finally, reconnect by disconnecting from your devices.** Turn off devices at meals. You need to be present with people. It is discourteous to be checking your texts or emails. The world functioned well before all of these devices were invented. Everything is not urgent. Learn to be present with people and the payoff will be deeper relationships, deeper business connections, and longer lasting and more fulfilling connections.

Key Words

Success	Disconnect	Rediscover
Release	Value	Self
Freedom	Integration	Others
Interaction	Be present	Family
Interconnected	Connection	Friendship
Time	Relationship	Emerge

Study Guide

I hope you have enjoyed reading The Woman Code paperback edition. As I said in the prologue to the book, these Codes have served me well throughout my life's journey. And I am certain that they will serve me well throughout the rest of my days.

The truth is, however, that there are literally dozens of Codes and virtues recognized throughout the world that could also be applied to our lives. I could only choose twenty for this book, and most of them came directly from life lessons I learned watching my paternal grandmother, Dora Nelson.

What I have tried to do in The Woman Code is to give you a roadmap for what I like to call the primary Codes or core Codes of living. These are commonsense, easy to engage principles that go to the core of our character and, most importantly, our ability to be "coachable," as my friend Dr. Sabrina Jackson likes to say.

This book is tailor-made to help engage women from all walks of life and all ages. Starting with our senior year in high school, up through college, into our career-building and child-raising stage, and then continuing on into midlife and our golden years. Whether you are a young woman just starting out or if, like me, you find yourself at midlife or older, you nevertheless likely need to learn or rediscover these core Codes of womanhood. They will help you to navigate your life and live it peacefully, powerfully, and purposely.

This study guide serves as just that—a guide: I suggest that you use it individually or in a small group setting. The questions and action-oriented steps will better help you to apply the "Codes" and the "keys" to unlock your life. More detailed questions and activities can be found at www.thewomancodebook.com.

Section I: The Personal Codes: Whatever is going on inside of you is what will come out of you. These four Codes are the foundation of every woman's life. All roads to positive life transformation begins with you doing the work on yourself. Self-examination is core to how we develop into the women we all want to be.

Code 1: Know Your Value

Code 2: Make Peace with Your Past

Code 3: Teach People How to Treat You

Code 4: Live Authentically

1. What does it mean to know your value?
2. How can we erase the negative tapes of our childhood or past experiences that made us feel valueless?
3. What painful and problematic thing from your past have you not dealt with because you are afraid to go there or open that wound?
4. Where do you find your worth and value?
5. Do you find it hard to let go of things or release things in your past? What holds you back?
6. Are you keeping secrets that you need to release from your spirit? How can you release these secrets and move forward?
7. How do you teach people to treat you at work, at home, at church, in your social interactions? Identify the ways in which you think people view you positively or negatively. Then write down how people see you treat yourself.
8. How do you define being authentic? How does the author define being authentic? How are the two definitions alike or different?
9. Do you struggle with being transparent, open, and authentic about who you really are behind the mask we all wear to show people our "best" selves?

10. What did you think of section I? Are the four personal Codes new to you? Identify several areas you feel you need to work on.

Section II: The Emotional Codes: Our emotions as women are at times both a blessing and a curse. These four Codes will help women to recognize and better manage our emotions from a place of wisdom, self-reflection, self-love, and resilience.

Code 5: Be Accountable for Your Life

Code 6: Guard Your Heart

Code 7: Be Resilient

Code 8: Age Gracefully

1. How can you be better accountable in your day-to-day life? Did you find the keys in Code 5 useful toward helping you to get there?
2. What does it mean to you to guard your heart? How does it match up with what you learned in Code 5?
3. Broken heart syndrome is real and people die from it every year. What habits will you put into practice to avoid the potential effects of broken heart syndrome?
4. The author says, *"Resilience* may be the most important word in the human vocabulary after love." Do you agree? Why or why not?
5. How do you feel about aging? Even if you are in your twenties now, how are you taking care of your mind, body, and soul to live better?

Section III: The Spiritual Codes: Every woman has a spirit. The spirit part of us is often the part we neglect most. Spirit is not religion. Spirit is not a bunch of rules. Spirit is what keeps you on track to nourish your soul and be a light to all who come across your path. These four Codes are simple, but they are powerful when put into practice in your daily life.

Code 9: Do Not Gossip

Code 10: Apologize Quickly

Code 11: Choose Your Thoughts and Words Wisely

Code 12: Never Cut What You Can Untie

1. Have you ever had someone gossip about you, whether their words were true or untrue? How did it feel?
2. Discuss in your groups whether or not it is ever okay to gossip and if there is such a thing as harmless gossip.
3. Code 9 is designed to help you to better understand what gossip is, how it works, and why it is so damaging to other women when we engage in it. Discuss what you learned from the personal story the author shared.
4. Why do you think the author says, "Apologize quickly"?
5. Make a list of people you may need to apologize to and find a way to offer an apology. Then make a list of who owes you an apology. Forgive those people and release them from their offense.
6. Why do you think it's important that we choose our thoughts and words both intentionally and carefully?
7. "Never cut what you can untie" is a powerful admonition. What does it mean to you to cut someone off or to untie from them?
8. In what ways did Code 12 make you see the value in untying from some people versus cutting them off for good?

Section IV: The Professional Codes: Successful women are intentional. They live by powerful Codes that integrate their personal, spiritual, and professional values into a winning strategy for all. They lead at work as they do at home: with heart, compassion, sisterhood, smarts, and savvy. That is what makes women unique.

Code 13: Don't Think Like a Man

Code 14: Lead from Within

Code 15: Be Brave

Code 16: Lift Other Women as You Climb

1. Why is it important for us as women to think like women and not like men?

2. Do you agree with the author that we can *learn* a lot from men, but that we should never try to act like or be men in the workplace or in dating relationships? Why or why not?

3. Go online and take an emotional IQ survey. There are many different ones. If you're doing this study with a group, share your emotional IQ with the group and identify areas in which you may need to improve.

4. Why do you think the author made the distinction between "being brave" and "being courageous"? Do you agree or disagree? What did you learn in Code 15?

5. Why do you think the author described sisterhood as an action word versus just a nice way of seeing other women?

6. Why should sisterhood matter to us collectively as women?

7. Give examples of how you can lift other women in your day-to-day life and in the workplace.

8. Make a commitment to stay connected to your circle of influence and women friends at least once per month socially outside of work to strengthen the bonds of sisterhood.

Section V: The Relational Codes: If COVID -19 has taught us anything --we know that we are in this life together. We are connected. We need one another. No Codes determine our ultimate joy, happiness, and fulfillment in life more than the Codes for how we relate to other people. At the end of the day, it is our relationships that make our lives worth living.

Code 17: Know Your Front Row

Code 18: Practice Love, Laughter, Loyalty

Code 19: Have Courageous Conversations

Code 20: Reconnect with Your Life

1. What priority do you place on having the right people in your life circle?

2. Discuss your reactions or thoughts on the author's analogy to a movie theater with seats and rows and that this is how we need to place people in our lives.

3. What did you think of Code 17, and how can you use it to help you grow as a person?

4. Love. Laughter. Loyalty. The author says these three *mini Codes* are crucial to the joy and fulfillment of our lives. Do you agree? If so, why, and if not, why not? What other mini Codes would you add to these three?

5. What does it mean to you to have a courageous conversation?

6. How has social media disconnected us as opposed to making us more connected? Discuss this and give examples of why you agree or disagree with the author's assessment in Code 19.

7. How do you take care of yourself on a regular basis?

8. How do you connect daily with friends and loved ones?

9. How do you define connection?

10. Describe how you want to reconnect your life to the things that matter when it comes to: Your soul. Your loved ones. Your passions. Your hobbies. Your dreams.

BONUS: Now review all the Codes and discuss how they fit together. Did you notice that if one Code is out of balance, another Code could be in jeopardy? Discuss which Codes you find to be the most difficult to manage and the ones you find much easier to embrace. This will help you to see the areas in which you need to do the most work. It could be in the emotional section, or it may be in the professional section. Find the courage to face your fears and work through them. This book was written so that we could unlock our inner greatness and help other women to do the same.

Notes

Code 2 Make Peace with Your Past

1. Elisabeth Kübler-Ross, *On Death and Dying* (New York: Scribner, 1969).

Code 4 Live Authentically

1. Polly Campbell, "5 Ways to Live an Authentic Life," Gaiam Life, http://life.gaiam.com/article/5-ways-live-authentic-life.

2. Michael Kernis and Brian Goldman, "The Role of Authenticity in Healthy Psychological Functioning and Subjective Well-Being," *Annals of the American Psychotherapy Association* 5 (November–December 2002).

Code 5 Be Accountable for Your Life

1. *Wikipedia*, s.v. "humility," http://en.wikipedia.org/wiki/Humility.

2. Proverbs 27:6.

3. W. Todd Smith, "Personal Accountability—A Requirement for Life Advancement," Little Things Matter, http://www.littlethingsmatter.com/blog/2010/10/07/personal-accountability%E2%80%94a-requirement-for-life-advancement.

Code 6 Guard Your Heart

1. Proverbs 4:23 WEB.

2. "Is Broken Heart Syndrome Real?" American Heart Association, April 15, 2013, http://www.heart.org/HEARTORG/Conditions/More/Cardiomyopathy/Is-Broken-Heart-Syndrome-Real_UCM_448547_Article.jsp.

3. American Heart Association, "Angina Pectoris/Stable Angina," http://www.heart.org/HEARTORG/Conditions/HeartAttack/SymptomsDiagnosisofHeartAttack/Angina-Pectoris-Stable-Angina_UCM_437515_Article.jsp.

4. American Heart Association, "Is Broken Heart Syndrome Real?" April 15, 2013, http://www.heart.org/HEARTORG/Conditions/More/Cardiomyopathy/Is-Broken-Heart-Syndrome-Real_UCM_448547_Article.jsp.

5. Henri J. M. Nouwen, *The Inner Voice of Love* (New York: Random House, 1996), 59.

6. Sophia A. Nelson, "After 9/11, One Man's Journey from Loss to Love," September 11, 2011, http://thegrio.com/2011/09/11/after-911-one-mans-journey-from-loss-to-love. Used with permission.

7. Michael Hyatt, "Three Reasons Why You Must Guard Your Heart," *Michael Hyatt: Helping Leaders Leverage Influence* (blog), May 16, 2011, http://michael hyatt.com/three-reasons-why-you-must-guard-your-heart.html.

Code 7 Be Resilient

1. Rande Iaboni, "L'Wren Scott Leaves $9 Million Estate to Mick Jagger," March 28, 2014, http://www.cnn.com/2014/03/27/showbiz/new-york-lwren-scott-estate/index.html.

2. Al Siebert, *The Resiliency Advantage* (San Francisco: Berrett-Koehler, 2005), 2.

3. Carolyn Gregoire, "How to Bounce Back from Failure—Over and Over Again," *The Huffington Post*, September 2, 2013, http://www.huffingtonpost.com/2013/09/02/habits-of-resilient-people_n_3818652.html.

4. Al Siebert, "Resiliency Quiz—How Resilient Are You?" Resiliency Center, http://www.resiliencycenter.com/resiliencyquiz.shtml. Permission has been granted for the use of this survey.

Code 8 Age Gracefully

1. Louise Hay, *Heal Your Body A-Z: The Mental Causes for Physical Illness and How to Overcome Them* (Carlsbad, CA: Hay House, 1998).

2. See http://www.psychpage.com/family/brwaitgalligher.html; http://longevity.about.com/od/lifelongrelationships/p/sex_longevity.htm; http://www.psychology today.com/blog/memory-medic/201307/does-humor-make-you-live-longer; http://www.webmd.com/food-recipes/features/antioxidants-in-green-and-black-tea; http://www.onsponge.com/articles/development/150-health-matters/381-healthy-mouth-can-prolong-your-life.

3. Matthew McConaughey said this at the 2014 Oscars.

Code 9 Do Not Gossip

1. "Sisters, It's Time to Heal," *Essence*, April 13, 2012, http://www.essence.com/2012/04/13/get-lifted-sisters-its-time-to-heal-part-i.

2. *Oxford Dictionaries*, s.v. "gossip," http://www.oxforddictionaries.com/us/definition/american_english/gossip.

3. See http://www.gotquestions.org/gossip-Bible.html.

4. According to http://www.bibleed.com/bibleteachings/otherbibleteachings/devil.asp, the word for *devil* is strictly New Testament and is the Greek *diablos*, meaning a "false accuser" or "slanderer," while *Satan* is a Hebrew word meaning "an enemy."

5. Zak Stambor, "Bonding Over Others' Business," *American Psychological Association*, April 2006, http://www.apa.org/monitor/apr06/bonding.aspx.

6. Cécile Guéret, "Why We Love to Gossip," Psychologies, December 7, 2011, https://psychologies.co.uk/self/why-we-love-to-gossip.html.

7. Rosemary Black, "10 Reasons Why Women Love to Gossip," Quality Health, May 13, 2010, http://www.qualityhealth.com/relationships-articles/10-reasons-why-women-love-gossip. Used by permission.

Code 10 Apologize Quickly

1. Charlene Laino, "Health Benefits of a Sincere Apology," WebMD, http://www.webmd.com/women/features/health-benefits-of-sincere-apology; Alison Turner, "Why Can't I Forgive? Top 8 Health Benefits of Forgiveness," Zoom Health, December 24, 2013, http://www.zoomhealth.net/WhyCan'tIForgive-Top8Health BenefitsofForgiveness.html.

2. Gary Chapman, *The Five Languages of Apology* (Chicago: Northfield Publishing, 2006), 16–18.

Code 11 Choose Your Thoughts and Words Wisely

1. Proverbs 18:21 VOICE.

2. "Feeling Our Emotions," *Scientific American*, March 24, 2005, http://www.scientificamerican.com/article/feeling-our-emotions.

3. Sy Kraft, "Love Study: Brain Reacts to Heartbreak Same as Physical Pain," Medical News Today, March 28, 2011, http://www.medicalnewstoday.com/articles/220427.php. See also David DiSalvo, "More Die of Heartbreak, More Often Than You Might Think," *Forbes*, October 3, 2012, http://www.forbes.com/sites/daviddisalvo/2012/10/03/more-die-of-heartbreak-more-often-than-you-might-think.

4. Recent studies, including a few especially compelling ones conducted at Johns Hopkins University and published in the *New England Journal of Medicine*, have confirmed the findings: a person's risk of death from heart attack significantly increases following a loved one's death. In one study, researchers tracked 1.5 million people between ages 35 and 84, and found that in the six months after losing a spouse, the risk of dying from a heart attack increased by 20 to 35 percent.

5. Elizabeth Gilbert, *Eat, Pray, Love* (New York: Viking, 2006), 178.

6. See Proverbs 18:21.

7. Luke 6:45.

Code 12 Never Cut What You Can Untie

1. Maya Angelou, "Maya Angelou Quotes," ThinkExist.com, http://thinkexist.com/quotation/i-ve_learned_that_people_will_forget_what_you/341107.html.

2. Nicole Roberts Jones, in discussion with the author, January 22, 2014.

Code 13 Don't Think Like a Man

1. See John and Stasi Eldredge, *Captivating* (Nashville: Thomas Nelson, 2005).

2. Aminu Abubakar and Josh Levs, "'I Will Sell Them,' Boko Haram Leader Says of Kidnapped Nigerian Girls," CNN, May 6, 2014, http://www.cnn.com/2014/05/05/world/africa/nigeria-abducted-girls.

3. Ben Spencer, "The Picture That Reveals Why Men and Women's Brains Really ARE Different," December 3, 2013, http://www.dailymail.co.uk/sciencetech/article-2516990/Sorry-chaps-brains-arent-multi-tasking-But-women-hard-wired-juggle-jobs.html.

4. Jason Howerton, "The Difference Between Men and Women's Brains Revealed?" The Blaze, December 2, 2013, http://www.theblaze.com/stories/2013/12/02/the-difference-between-men-and-womens-brains-revealed-in-this-photo.

Code 14 Lead from Within

1. "The Shriver Report: A Woman's Nation Pushes Back from the Brink," Newsvine, http://redsfan.newsvine.com/_news/2014/01/12/22278428-the-shriver-report-a-womans-nation-pushes-back-from-the-brink. Used by permission.

2. Jeanne Meister, "Job Hopping Is the 'New Normal' for Millennials: Three Ways to Prevent a Human Resource Nightmare," Forbes, August 14, 2012, http://www.forbes.com/sites/jeannemeister/2012/08/14/job-hopping-is-the-new-normal-for-millennials-three-ways-to-prevent-a-human-resource-nightmare/.

Code 15 Be Brave

1. Mark Twain, "Mark Twain Quotes," ThinkExist.com, http://thinkexist.com/quotation/courage_is_resistance_to_fear-mastery_of_fear-not/177585.html.

Code 16 Lift Other Women as You Climb

1. Sophia A. Nelson, "Time to Put the 'Sister' Back in 'Sisterhood,'" The Huffington Post, December 11, 2013, http://www.huffingtonpost.com/sophia-a-nelson/what-is-sisterhood-really_b_4410051.html.

2. See http://www.oprah.com/oprahshow/Oprah-and-Iyanla-Vanzants-Misunderstanding-Video.

Code 17 Know Your Front Row

1. Colin Powell, "Colin Powell Quotes," GoodReads, http://www.goodreads.com/author/quotes/138507.Colin_Powell.

2. Proverbs 27:6.

Code 18 Practice Love, Laughter, Loyalty

1. Proverbs 17:22.

2. William James, "William James Quotes," ThinkExist.com, http://thinkexist.com/quotation/we_don-t_laugh_because_we-re_happy-we-re_happy/342801.html.

3. Jeanne Segal and Melinda Smith, "Laughter Is the Best Medicine," Help Guide.org, April 2014, http://www.helpguide.org/life/humor_laughter_health.htm.

4. "2009 Men's Dating Trends," AskMen.com, http://www.askmen.com/specials/2009-great-male-survey.

5. Brené Brown, "Quotes about Shame," Goodreads, http://www.goodreads.com/quotes/tag/shame.

Code 19 Have Courageous Conversations

1. *The Free Dictionary*, s.v. "conversation," http://www.thefreedictionary.com/conversation.

2. Laurie Gerber, "Hard Conversations: How to Tackle Them Head-On," *The Huffington Post*, January 26, 2011, http://www.huffingtonpost.com/laurie-gerber/hard-conversations-how-to-tackle-them_b_813730.html.

Sophia A. Nelson, Esq., is an award-winning journalist, frequent on-air political commentator for CNN, and adjunct professor of religion and philosophy at Christopher Newport University. She is the author of three bestselling nonfiction books: the award-winning *Black Woman Redefined: Dispelling Myths and Discovering Fulfillment in the Age of Michelle Obama* (2011); *The Woman Code: 20 Powerful Keys to Unlock Your Life* (2014 and 2021); and *ePluribus ONE: Reclaiming Our Founders' Vision for a United America* (2017). Nelson is a highly sought-after motivational speaker and leadership trainer in Fortune 500 companies and at colleges and universities all over the world. She is a senior columnist for *USA Today* and contributing editor at *theGrio.com*, and writes frequently for *The Washington Post, Politico Magazine, The New York Daily News,* and *BET News.*